DISCARD

WALKING DISTANCE

PILGRIMAGE,

PARENTHOOD,

WALKING

MICHIGAN STATE UNIVERSITY PRESS | *East Lansing*

GRIEF,

DISTANCE

AND HOME REPAIRS

DAVID HLAVSA

⊗ The paper used in this publication meets the minimum requirements
of ANSI/NISO Z39.48-1992 (R 1997) (Permanence of Paper).

Michigan State University Press
East Lansing, Michigan 48823-5245

Printed and bound in the United States of America.

21   20   19   18   17   16   15   1   2   3   4   5   6   7   8   9   10

Library of Congress Control Number: 2015934735
ISBN: 978-1-61186-186-0 (pbk.)
ISBN: 978-1-60917-473-6 (ebook: PDF)
ISBN: 978-1-62895-245-2 (ebook: ePub)
ISBN: 978-1-62896-245-1 (ebook: Kindle)

Book design by Charlie Sharp, Sharp Des!gns, Lansing, Michigan
Cover design by Shaun Allshouse, www.shaunallshouse.com
Cover photograph is used courtesy of David Hlavsa. All rights reserved.

Michigan State University Press is a member of the Green Press Initiative and is committed
to developing and encouraging ecologically responsible publishing practices. For more
information about the Green Press Initiative and the use of recycled paper in book
publishing, please visit *www.greenpressinitiative.org*.

Visit Michigan State University Press at *www.msupress.org*

For Lisa

Everywhere is within walking distance
if you have the time.

—STEVEN WRIGHT

ACKNOWLEDGMENTS

The plainest fact is: I married well.

When it comes to this book, my wife, Lisa Holtby, did everything but write it. The story is one in which a lot happens to Lisa, so what you may not realize from reading it is how much Lisa is a person who *makes* things happen. I write about a time in our marriage when Lisa was forced to depend on me, and so this book does not—not nearly—give the reader a sense of how much I depend on her.

It's not just that Lisa planned the trip to Spain, walked the miles, found and helped to renovate the house, and bore the children; when I first started writing about the experience of losing James, it was Lisa who suggested that people might want to read it. I demurred, but she persisted until I sent it in to the "Modern Love" column of the *New York Times*. Having that first article published led to offers to write other articles, which led me to suspect I had a book on my hands. Throughout, Lisa was a formidable and tireless editor, going over the various drafts of the book word by word, asking good questions, making suggestions, and gently (okay, sometimes not so gently) reining in my rhetorical excesses. All this while doing more than her share of the housework and child-rearing so that I could have time to write while still keeping my day job. And then, once I had a full manuscript, Lisa set the vision for getting it out to a wider audience.

She held my hand and coached me through the process of designing a website, writing query letters, getting rejected, and finally finding an agent and a publisher.

This is a hard book to categorize—it's part travel book, part home-repair saga, part meditation on grief, but more than anything, I wrote it as a love letter to my wife, and I hope that's how it reads.

Many thanks to Dani Shapiro and to my agent, Sam Stoloff of the Frances Goldin Literary Agency, for their enthusiastic support and for taking a chance on me; to the reviewers at Michigan State University Press for their detailed and useful critiques of the manuscript; to Olivia Archibald, Jeff Birkenstein, and the students in our creative writing class, who all gave good feedback on early drafts; to Dan Jones of the *Times* for seeing the real story under the story I'd written; to my mother, Vivi Hlavsa, for her enthusiastic fandom, her insightful comments, and for teaching me to write in the first place; and, for advice and counsel, to Janel Atlas, Fred Albert, Ven. Dhammadinna, Henry Burton, David Hsieh, Andrea Allen, Holly Harmon, Joe Shirley, Kathleen Pape, Gabriella Möller, Ann Pelo, Beverly Harding Buehler, Gary Luke of Sasquatch Press, Meg Storey of Tinhouse Press, Jennifer McCord of Coffeetown Press, and Priscilla Long. It's been a long road; thanks to all who helped us along and apologies to anyone I've neglected here.

WALKING DISTANCE

Near the beginning of the medieval morality play *Everyman*, Death walks up to Everyman with the message that Everyman must go on a pilgrimage. Death is a stranger to him, so it takes a while for Everyman to understand what is happening and to *get* the message; he's been living his life the way most of us do, preoccupied with making a living, getting along, trying to get more of what he enjoys and to avoid what he doesn't. Absorbed in the everyday numbing push and pull of craving and aversion, Everyman is so unmindful of the very existence of Death that he does not recognize him; he makes fun of Death, this religious fanatic who thinks he has a message from God. But then something Death says or does—it's not clear what—brings Everyman up short, and he *sees*.

"Oh, *Death*," he says.

Everyman begs for some respite, a chance to put his affairs in order. Given the state of his affairs, he figures it should only take about twelve years or so. But Death says: No, you have no more time.

So Everyman pleads for Death to give him a day, just one day. He tells Death he isn't ready.

Death says: No, you have no more time.

Everyman asks: If I go on this pilgrimage, can I come back?

Death says: No.

Everyman asks: Can I at least have someone come with me?

Death says, in essence: Sure. Good luck finding someone. I'll be right back.

Everyman has the simplest of plots: as he makes his way to the grave, Everyman tries to find someone or something that will endure the journey and keep him company. Death has given him no time, and Everyman's pilgrimage takes place in that moment: God's time, all time and no time at all.

And it is in this urgent moment, thrust into this suddenly purposeful journey, and in the fullness of his grief, that Everyman realizes that his previous life was no life at all, and that what he needs in the end is the kind of true companionship you can find only in service to others. At the very edge of the grave, Everyman comes alive.

HOME

1.

In the summer of the year 2000, Lisa and I walked the Camino de Santiago, the Way of Saint James, more than four hundred miles across the north of Spain from the Pyrenees to Santiago de Compostela. Shortly after our return, Lisa got pregnant. James was the only name we considered for a boy. Inasmuch as anything can prepare you for a birth, I suppose walking the Camino prepared us for his. And inasmuch as anything can prepare anyone, it prepared us for his death as well.

Unlike Everyman's decision to go on pilgrimage, ours was neither involuntary nor did it happen all at once. Its arrival in our lives was not particularly momentous. There was no vision, no visitation. Nobody fell off a donkey. One day, in the tenth year of our marriage, Lisa and I were baking on a beach in the Caribbean. White sand, palms, light breeze, turquoise water, eighty degrees. We had good jobs: I had recently received tenure as a theater professor; Lisa was bringing in good money as a yoga teacher. We had some savings and a small co-op apartment in a hip Seattle neighborhood. No more low-budget road trips, car camping, sleeping on college friends' couches, standby flights; these days, we could afford a real grown-up vacation.

The beach was full of sand fleas, and I was starting to burn. I'm not really a beach kind of person, and I hate being a tourist—a visitor, isolated, surrounded by the vibrant life of a tropical island with no real way to be a part of it. Vacations and holidays have always been restless times for me. Something in me says: Why vacate? Why go on a retreat? I don't want to retreat; I want to advance. Instead, there we were: beached.

Of course, vacation wasn't the problem; the problem was me. It wasn't just that I was bored; any time I wasn't at work, I struggled with a combination of low-level anxiety and depression, a slight but perceptible dissociation from my domestic life, as if I had been given a mild sedative and could never quite emerge fully from its speedy, torpid blur.

At work, which, for a teacher, is infinitely expandable, I had classes to plan, students to cajole, committees to chair, resources to marshal, artists to collaborate with, deadlines, challenges. Add to these preoccupations the cycle of producing plays: each new cast a community forged in the attempt to make something fine, each rehearsal period a brief lifetime unto itself, and each closing night the end of a world. It's not that I was always happy at work, but when you get in the habit of trying to fill the hole in your heart with professional achievements, if you're any good at what you do, there's always just enough of a kick to the workday to keep you coming back for more.

Lisa once said accusingly, "I think you like being at work a lot better than being at home." I thought about trying to reassure her that it wasn't so, but then I just nodded. She had me there.

During our courtship, I had wooed her with an old-fashioned fervor that, fortunately for me, she found charming—if sometimes a little overwhelming. Like a lot of men I know, I could be very good at the initial pursuit, but once I got the girl, I wasn't quite sure what to do with her. However hard I tried to be a good husband, it seemed there was always a part of me disengaged from the action of marriage, the shared effort of making a life together. I was at home at work and a tourist in my home.

I rolled over on my towel and muttered something to Lisa about wishing our time off from work had more of a sense of purpose.

Sometimes a simple remark just unfolds and unfolds. At first it looks like any other wrinkled scrap of thought. But then, as you smooth it out, it expands impossibly, all out of proportion. You want to see it in full, so you start to push other things aside to accommodate it. At first the unfolding seems like a game, an absurd magic trick, but then it takes up the whole room, and you stare at what's before you, stunned: you realize it's a map of the territory ahead.

I trace my very existence back to a simple remark. My parents were in college, still in their teens; my father, a tall, gangly, quiet kid who liked to play basketball as long as no one took the game too seriously, and my mother, curvy, dark-haired, intense in her convictions, were midway through a conversation about something else when he turned to her and, so the story goes, blurted out, "So, do you want to get married or *not*?"

So, having arrived at this very comfortable place in our lives, where *did* Lisa and I want to go from here, and what would make the journey more purposeful? When we got home from the Caribbean, we started to reconsider not just our vacation plans, but our destinations in general. Marriage, like pregnancy, is both an either/or proposition and a work in progress. How married were we? We both felt we could be more married. My tolerance for intimacy, for instance: Lisa opined that it might be a good idea for me to make some improvements in that area. And I replied that such an improvement should probably be accompanied by an expansion of Lisa's tolerance for, well, *me*—which, though it had markedly increased in recent years, was still, by my standards, far too limited.

Over the years, we had fought plenty, but clearly there were some battles we were avoiding. And we had decisions to make. Our childlessness, for example, was one indicator that our marriage could use some work—not the fact of childlessness itself, but our irresolution over it.

From the beginning, we had shifted back and forth about having a baby. On one of our first dates, we were sitting side by side on a park bench, and she said that she doubted she would ever want children. I understood that it was a casual remark—and I wasn't sure I wanted children either—but I didn't want to close off the option. So, rather than letting the remark pass, I told her that if she definitely didn't want children, I wasn't sure we ought to be seeing each other. Lisa looked a bit startled—after all, we barely knew each other—and then she moved a little closer to me on the bench. Sure I was a little goofy, but maybe I had potential.

By our midthirties, Lisa had changed her mind; she wanted a child, and soon. I didn't think I was ready. For one thing, though I had limited experience with them, I wasn't particularly keen on children. They seemed to like to climb on me, and I found that kind of flattering, but that didn't mean I wanted one. Lisa didn't push me. I pretended to be in the question for a while, but how do you make a decision like that? I could make a list of pluses and minuses, but who was I kidding? There was no way to make a rational determination. It didn't feel right to just say no, so I just said yes.

I'd said it on Maui, two years before, on another beach vacation, as Lisa and I stood on the summit of Haleakalā, watching the sun rise from the ocean and set the volcanic moonscape below us on fire. I pictured myself with a child on my lap saying, "Junior, did I ever tell you about the moment you first became a gleam in your old man's eye?"

Later, as we were hiking down the slope of the mountain, Lisa slipped and cut her shin on the rough volcanic rock. She still has a bit of a scar—it looked as if she'd taken a large cheese grater to her leg. Though she made it to the bottom of the trail okay, her sock and sneaker were soaked with blood, and all along the way she drew horrified stares from the other hikers we encountered.

I'm sure some people pass from the practice of contraception to the practice of conception easily, like a man stripping off his necktie on a hot Friday afternoon—Oh, thank God, I don't have to wear *that* any more. I remember speculating that although having a child would undoubtedly disrupt our future sex life, we could now, for a limited time only, enjoy a stretch of pure liberation, sex whenever we wanted and no fooling with diaphragms or gels or condoms or all the other paraphernalia we'd seen as standard equipment in our reasonably responsible respective sexual histories.

But the sex that night was oddly tentative, giddy and terrifying, as if we'd been transported back to our teens. We fumbled around, the tension broken every now and then by one of us bursting out laughing and then saying something like, "Sorry, sorry. No really. Continue. As you were."

(We did eventually get our groove back, thanks for asking.)

After a couple of months of haphazard attempts, Lisa took on the new pregnancy project in earnest, charting her cycle, taking her temperature, and reading up on the best ways to increase our chances, including, as one article put it, making gravity work for *you*! One time, afterward, for good measure, my wife the yoga teacher got out of bed and, naked and giggling madly, did a few minutes in headstand.

"So what do you call that in Sanskrit?" I asked.

Every so often, Lisa would call me at work with the news: "I'm ovulating! Hurry home!" And I'd reply, "Yes ma'am, at your service." Later that evening, I'd tell her that, in the middle of the afternoon faculty meeting, I'd considered leaping up and, before dashing from the room, intoning, "Please excuse me. With all due respect, I've got to go impregnate my wife now."

In time, when we had failed to conceive by conventional means, we sought medical advice. It turned out that my sperm, though sufficiently numerous, included a disconcerting proportion of anomalies: benighted tadpoles swimming mightily in circles, microscopic push-me-pull-yous with two tails, and the just plain dead. Clearly, the problem was with me, but, as is often the case, it was Lisa who paid. Following the doctors' regimen, each month I was provided with a plastic specimen cup, a pleasant enough little private room, and access to pornography. Lisa's part was to receive regular, painful shots in the ass with fertility drugs, to lie on the doctor's table for the monthly turkey-basting, and then, to turn inwards, exquisitely aware of every sign and tide of her body, until the next disappointment. Start over.

Like a lot of people in our part of the world, Lisa and I are unchurched (though I was raised Quaker). Spiritually eclectic, we've each practiced a number of different varieties of meditation and prayer. Praying comes naturally to Lisa—it's just something she's always done. It's not a mystical experience, she tells me; she's not hearing voices or seeing auras or what have you. She simply prays, as one might converse with a friend—if that friend happened to be infinitely loving and utterly unknowable. My experience is not so direct. It's not that I'm devoid of religious feeling or belief, but when I try to pray in words—whether silently or aloud—I usually just feel self-conscious, as if I'm shouting into a toy telephone in the hope of getting a voice on the other end of the line.

But, most of the time, that doesn't stop me from trying to connect. One New Year's Eve, we sat in a hotel room in Portland and wrote invitations to a child to join us. I pictured a large, well-appointed room somewhere in limbo, babies of all sorts and colors, lounging on velvety pillows, coyly waiting for a sufficiently compelling summons to go and be born. Lisa's invitation had a lot to do with how much we wanted to be loving parents. Mine was a list, in no particular order, of incentives to come to this world: cake, Otis Redding, falling in love, hummingbirds, home, Swiss army knives, those kinds of things.

After nearly three years of trying to conceive a child, I wanted to continue, but Lisa had had enough. We fought to an uneasy cease-fire, and then settled into a tacit agreement to leave it be. And there it sat in our apartment: the *it* we had left be. We hauled it with us to the Caribbean that winter where it sat glumly between us on the beach until we were ready to drag it on home. Though we certainly didn't want to talk about it anymore, clearly trying to have a child had separated us in an important way, and whether we eventually became parents or not, we were looking for inspiration, for a joint enterprise to bring us back together.

And then, one Sunday afternoon, Lisa looked up from the travel section of the *New York Times* and asked me if I'd ever heard of the Camino de Santiago.

■   ■   ■

The Camino, the Way of Saint James, began in the ninth century when the bones of the apostle were discovered in northwestern Spain. The legend was that after the Crucifixion, James, the first of Christ's followers, traveled to Spain for his ministry. When he returned to Judea and was eventually martyred there, his compatriots took his body back to Spain by boat and interred it in the Roman burial ground of Compostela.

Upon the miraculous rediscovery of the bones in 813 AD, people began to come to Spain in increasing numbers, reaching half a million—and by some estimates as many as two million—per year by the thirteenth century. The oldest of the established pathways, the Camino Francés, winds through the northern Pyrenees, passes through Pamplona and the Basque country to Burgos, across the high plains to León, and over two mountain ridges, the Montes de León and the Sierra de Ancares, to Galicia.

Pilgrimage was the forerunner of modern tourism; one of the first written tour guides, the *Codex Calixtinus*, comes from the early days of the Camino. Shrines, churches, inns, and whole towns sprang up along the way. Pilgrims—in Spanish, *peregrinos*—came on foot, on horseback, and by ship from all over the Christian world. They made the journey, which was both arduous and dangerous, interrupted their lives for months, because they believed in miracles, because they needed to do penance for their sins, because pilgrimage frees the soul from purgatory.

Then, if they survived, they turned around and walked, rode, sailed back home. And their lives were different. Their communities expected more of them, and they expected more from themselves. Some changed their names to reflect the fact that they had traveled the Way of Saint James. Perhaps for some it was just a status symbol, but for others the name change was no doubt meant to convey true transformation. In some important sense, they had never returned from the pilgrimage; they were still on the Camino.

We decided that this was the experience we wanted—something that would extend well beyond the journey itself—and so we found ourselves contemplating not just a long trip but the long run. On our return from Spain, what kind of life were we hoping to lead? And—there it was again—would that life include children or not?

■　　■　　■

About the time we were gingerly reopening this discussion, Lisa began giving private yoga lessons to Claire. A longtime student of Lisa's, Claire had just lost both her children in the crash of Alaska Airlines Flight 261. Her daughters, Cori, age eight, and Blake, six, were flying home with their father and stepmother when the plane went down in the ocean off the coast of California killing all eighty-eight people on board. Claire and her ex-husband had a joint custody agreement; that week it was his turn to take the girls.

For many months after the crash, except for long walks, Claire rarely left her home, the walls plastered with the girls' drawings, the shelves full of family photos and memorabilia. People came to take care of her as best they could. She did get out to the yoga studio, however, where each week Lisa would lead Claire, her mother, her sisters, and her partner Marj through a private session. Claire told her that, along with walking, yoga was one of the few things that helped her get through the day.

Most of Lisa's students are high achievers—doctors, lawyers, businesspeople, activists—and Claire had been among them, a family physician with a thriving practice that she managed to schedule around caring for her daughters. Being a witness to such devastating grief effected a sea change in Lisa. She began to wonder: if losing a child can reduce such a life as Claire's to pure aftermath, what must it be like to love a child?

So it was that, in our minds, the Camino became a way to prepare ourselves for parenthood. We would use the pilgrimage as a way to deepen our spiritual lives and strengthen our marriage. On the road, we would spend part of each day in silent meditation, paying attention to each step, breathing, and listening for what the Quakers call the still small voice within. And at the end of each day, we would talk: about all the things married people defer, withhold, make quiet bargains not to speak of. We would clean out the closets, rid ourselves of the inevitable accumulation of detritus between us: judgments, resentments, fears, desires, shames, stratagems. We would try to be both more truthful and kinder to one another.

All these renovations, we believed, would make us better potential parents, and we had the idea that, as our potential increased, so would the likelihood of our becoming actual parents. I wouldn't say that our new notion of pilgrimage was quid pro quo—Okay, God: we walk, you hand over the baby. Nor did we believe that the pilgrimage was an atonement, that we were childless because of our past sins. But we did have the sense that just maybe, if we really prepared ourselves for the arrival of a child, a child might arrive. When we got back, we would make more room in our lives: we would build a better nest, move from our urban neighborhood, buy a house in a quiet residential area. And then, if we couldn't grow a baby ourselves, we would go out and start looking for one.

Sure, it was ambitious, but then, Lisa and I are planners. As a theater professor, I've always got something simmering on the back burner of my mind: shows, classes, and—as I actually enjoy faculty politics—the occasional, if small, coup d'état. However, my planning extends only to the medium range, a year into the future at most. Lisa, by contrast, lays out detailed, long-term visions in a journal, which, judging by the number of volumes we have stored in our basement, she has kept since about the age of eighteen months. And then there are the files. Every month Lisa receives various magazines and rifles through them, scissors flashing; she stores the neatly clipped and annotated remains in folders whose organization is utterly mysterious to me. Everything she has achieved or procured in her life has its antecedents in the journals and clipping files. I suspect that if I were to browse through the files she put together before we met, I would eventually find an artist's conception of my own face, with the handwritten caption: "Husband?"

■   ■   ■

As was the way in our marriage, Lisa immediately took on all the planning for the trip, and I did very little indeed. She signed up for Spanish lessons. She bought several books on the Camino and contentedly started marking them up, putting color-coded sticky tabs on important pages, of which there were many. She kitted us out with lightweight washable travel clothing, including broad-brimmed black hats, pants with zippers at the knee so they could be converted into shorts, special moisture-wicking socks, and so on.

While equipping us was going nicely enough, Lisa's efforts to learn Spanish ground painfully to a halt. She loved her teacher, a flamboyant (aren't all language teachers flamboyant?) Argentine woman who taught her to say "¡Miercoles!" (the Spanish equivalent of "shoot"—"shit" is *mierda*) when she stubbed a toe, say, or dropped a casserole. Or forgot her Spanish vocabulary—Lisa is a good student, the kind any teacher would dream about: punctual, friendly, eager to learn, polite, not afraid to try new things, a good sport. However, it soon became apparent that when it came to Spanish, she wasn't learning *miercoles*.

I had taken Spanish classes in both high school and college, learning enough to pass the tests and promptly forgetting it all as soon as I could. I was, at best, an indifferent student, at worst a study in passive aggression toward my teachers. My college roommate, Walter, was no help: he would write entirely fictitious personal essays for Spanish class that were as absurd as they were grammatically straightforward: "My family and I visit the museum of Norman Rockwell in Utica, New York, every year during the summer holidays. We like his paintings of children and dogs." I was a fan of this sort of creeping surrealism, and Walter was my hero.

But Lisa's stalling out in the language department was not just a hitch in our planning; it was an outright roadblock. The guidebooks had warned us that almost no one along the Camino speaks English. If we wanted to find our way, if we wanted to eat, it would be Spanish or nothing. And then there was the matter of making hotel reservations. Strictly speaking, you don't need reservations to walk the Camino. Indeed, the majority of peregrinos stay in hostels or *refugios*. Maintained largely by volunteers, the refugios are inexpensive, and staying in them is a good way to experience the communal life of the road. Some are pleasant; others are rudimentary: cold showers, shared cooking areas, large sleeping rooms with bunk beds, people snoring.

Though Lisa was voted "Friendliest Girl" in seventh grade, neither of us is particularly gregarious. Both of us are only children, accustomed to a certain amount of solitude. In thinking about the trip, we weren't too worried by the prospect of a little physical discomfort, but we knew that consistently staying in communal housing would very quickly turn us to crabby peregrinos indeed. If we were going to walk all day, every day, we wanted some assurance there would be some quiet, private places to lie down. In order to accomplish that we would need to start composing faxes and making international phone calls in Spanish ("If you please, could we have your *quietest* room?"). Language wasn't Lisa's only frustration; she was overwhelmed at work, and perhaps just a little irritated by my dilatory participation in our preparations. With a flourish, I offered to take over all the planning for the trip and, to my chagrin, Lisa accepted. With a sigh of relief, she stepped down, and with more than a little sense of foreboding, I stepped up.

■ ■ ■

By this time, we knew the dates of the trip, and so I had a deadline: four months to learn a language, make travel arrangements, assemble our gear, get started on some serious talking about our relationship, and look for a neighborhood we'd like to raise a child in. And keep the day job. Check.

Then there was the matter of my feet: big, broad, flat as flounders, and subject to plantar fasciitis, which is Latin for the sensation of being repeatedly stabbed in the sole of one's foot with a salad fork. A doctor suggested that in order to avoid a bad episode on the trail, it would be best to work my way up slowly to within 10 percent of our planned weekly mileage. I worked it out with a calendar and a calculator: the week before we left, I should be walking about ninety miles per week, which works out to about thirteen miles or nearly four and a half hours of walking per day. Check.

Trying to solve all these problems simultaneously led to a kind of bizarre multitasking. I knew that Spanish classes wouldn't work for me, but I learn very well by ear. So I got language tapes from the library and studied Spanish as I walked about Seattle. Muttering to myself in tongues, looking for child-friendly neighborhoods, it's a wonder I wasn't arrested.

Sometimes Lisa would come with me. We'd lace up our boots, strap on our backpacks, and in keeping with our new program of having it all out, we would commence to fighting over present troubles and blaming each other for past ones. And then we would each imagine how the other might screw up our child in the future, and we'd fight about that. I would accuse her of controlling and overscheduling our poor hypothetical offspring; and she would counter by asking me when was I going to get more involved in theoretical-junior's education, and why didn't I do more work around the imaginary house? Most of it was fun; Lisa and I are good at making each other laugh. Then again, one time I made her so mad that she hauled off and slugged me.

■ ■ ■

All the world's major religions have their holy sites and their own pilgrimage traditions. As a Jew, as his forefathers had done, Christ traveled to the holy city of Jerusalem for Passover. His ministry, and the ministry of his apostles both before and after the Crucifixion, can be seen as pilgrimage: travel as an expression of faith. Christ urged his followers to take nothing with them but the barest of essentials; before him, the Buddha and, after him, Muhammad did the same. Saint Francis reportedly walked the Camino de Santiago naked.

While most peregrinos do not adopt quite such an ascetic lifestyle—taking along, at least, what Chaucer called the pilgrim's "bag of needments"—pilgrims of all faiths embrace a certain austerity born, if not of faith, of practicality: when you carry all your possessions on your back, they are quite literally a burden. The first pilgrims on the Camino evolved a kind of standard outfit: a cloak and a broad-brimmed hat to ward off sun and rain, a staff for stability and self-defense (until relatively recently, packs of wild dogs were a hazard), and a gourd to carry water in. Those returning from Santiago brought back scallop shells from the Spanish coast as souvenirs. The shell became the symbol of the pilgrimage and the one adornment to the peregrino's costume.

For the most part, when packing for a pilgrimage—as, to his dismay, Everyman discovers—you can't take it with you. Guidebooks advise the modern peregrino to limit his possessions to no more than 10 percent of his body weight. That meant that, between us, Lisa and I could carry about thirty-two pounds. Figuring in such needments as clothing, toiletries, sunscreen, medications, raingear, documents, maps, reading material, food and water, plus the weight of the packs themselves, we still exceeded the maximum needment allowance. After obsessing for some time over whether to bring a second pair of shoes, say, or a Spanish phrasebook, one day I caught myself actually contemplating boosting my gross weight in order to increase the net weight of my cargo. I was considering getting fat so that I could bring more stuff.

· · ·

The time for departure drew nearer. Plane tickets, traveler's checks, vaccinations . . . What had we forgotten? Credentials—better get some, we thought. We had our passports and such, but I had some lingering worry that people in Spain wouldn't accept us as pilgrims. According to the guidebooks, if you want to be recognized as a peregrino, at the beginning of your walk you ask at a church for a pilgrim's passport, a *credencial*, which allows you stay at the refugios. Along the route, you can get your credencial stamped at churches, hotels, restaurants, and *bars* (reading this, I pictured drunken peregrinos staggering across Spain in a protracted sacramental pub crawl). On arrival in Santiago, you present your documents to Church officials who—provided you have the stamps to prove you have walked at least the last hundred kilometers of the Camino—present you with a certificate called a *Compostela*. Pretty straightforward. However, according to one guidebook, in order to obtain a credencial, you need a letter of reference testifying to the seriousness of your spiritual intent.

This gave me pause. Was my intent sufficiently serious? If I walked to Mecca, I wouldn't presume to call myself a pilgrim. Where did I get the idea that it would be okay to go on a Catholic pilgrimage?

I've hung out with Catholics my whole life. I grew up in Queens, my Quaker family surrounded by Catholics. Each Christmas, our house was the only one not completely swathed in strands of multicolored blinking lights. No life-sized glowing Santa. No plastic reindeer on the roof. No crèche on the lawn complete with wise men, shepherds, cows, sheep, cupids and doves in midflight, and at the center, either the figure of baby Jesus himself or just the glow from a hidden sixty-watt bulb. At our house, to my great embarrassment, only a single tasteful WASP-y strand of blue and green lights on a lone pine.

My friends who didn't go to public school went to Saint Robert's; they came home with exciting tales of omniscient, ruler-wielding nuns, narrow escapes, children who were never seen again. One of their songs began, "Run, run, run—I think I hear a nun—pack up the liquor and run." And though I was happy at my Quaker elementary school, where everyone was just as nice as pie, I couldn't help but feel I was missing out on an adventure.

Perhaps it's no accident, then, that I teach at Saint Martin's, but there's no way you'd confuse me with a Catholic. I love the spectacle, the ritual of the Catholic mass, the call and response, the gestures, the maximum drama of the Transubstantiation of the Host. I love it the way my father (a lapsed Catholic), who always made fun of musicals, was actually a closet opera buff. The Mass moves me, and I attend now and again, but even if I'm really inspired, I know enough not to take Communion.

So how was going on a Catholic pilgrimage any less disrespectful than sneaking into the Communion line? I pictured us arriving in Spain: before we even walk the first hundred yards a guard stops us and orders us to say a Hail

Mary. We begin the prayer bravely, but falter after a line or two. A siren wails. We are exposed as impostors. "These two, they are not pilgrims," shouts the Inquisitor. "They are *tourists!*"

∎　　∎　　∎

One of the benefits of being on the faculty at Saint Martin's is that there is a community of Benedictine monks who pray for you several times a day. They founded the school in 1895, and though most of the classes are no longer taught by monks, they are a constant presence and force on campus, as tangible as gravity. A young man enters the monastery, renounces all his possessions, becomes part of the community, takes vows, lives by the Rule of Saint Benedict, works on the campus, grows old there, and when he dies he is buried there along with his brethren. It's a short walk from the monastery to the cemetery.

I made an appointment with the Abbot to ask him to write us a letter of reference. He showed me into his small office, and we sat in wing chairs by the unlit fireplace. Though it was springtime, there were still Christmas decorations on the mantelpiece. I'd never been to his office before—or even inside the monastery—and I felt as if I had been sent to see the principal. When he asked why we were going on the pilgrimage, I stammered a bit and finally blurted out that I wasn't sure I knew how to pray. "All I know how to do is listen," I said. He nodded. "That's a good start." He assured me that he'd write us the letter. I got up to leave, and as he stood to see me out, he gestured toward the Christmas decorations a little sheepishly. He shrugged. "I love Christmas," he said.

As my school year drew to a close, a last flurry of activity, putting our affairs in order, casting off the lines tethering us to our daily lives: keys to the neighbors, pay the bills, put the mail on hold. At their last yoga session, Claire gave Lisa a small string of beads, a token to carry with us in remembrance of Cori and Blake.

Then, one day, it's time to go.

AWAY

2.

We've chosen as our departure point the mountain village of Roncesvalles, on the Spanish side of the border with France. The town is not much more than a couple of bars, a refugio, and a small hotel. The evening before we start, there is a pilgrim mass in the medieval church. On the way in, we receive a card with the traditional Pilgrim's Blessing in Spanish. Flipping through my pocket dictionary while we're waiting for the mass to begin, I whisper to Lisa my rough translation:

> In the name of our savior, Jesus Christ, receive this knapsack, habit of your pilgrimage which will chastise and reform you as you hurry on foot to Santiago, where you long to arrive, and with which after having made your journey, you return to our side with joy, with God's help, who lives and reigns for all the centuries, amen. Receive this staff, may it sustain you on your walk and in your work, all the way of your pilgrimage; with it may you overcome the hordes of the enemy and come safely on foot to Santiago; and after making the journey, return together to us with happiness, with the blessing of that same God who lives and reigns for centuries of centuries, amen.

Or something like that. During the service, there is a sudden and violent storm, thunder following hard upon lightning. This seems to me a bit much, a little heavy on the foreshadowing, but then, how do I know what we're getting into? Hordes? None of the guidebooks mentioned hordes . . .

We begin walking on Lisa's thirty-fifth birthday, part of a small flock of peregrinos released at dawn, as if from a pigeon coop, onto the country road that passes through Roncesvalles. We're a little giddy, lightheaded, and light on our feet. The backpacks feel fine. Lisa loves her boots. We breakfast on a large Hershey bar with almonds (brought from home), my birthday present to Lisa. Most of the pilgrims around us look a little less shiny than we do, having begun the trip a couple of days ago on the French side of the border, at the base rather than the top of the mountain pass. Hanging on the backpacks of these relative veterans, the most common adornment is not the scallop shell but the true sign of the peregrino: the previous day's pair of damp socks.

The first day's walk is relatively undemanding. It is literally all downhill and, for now, not at the kind of punishing angle that leads to shin splints. We are relieved to find that it's not at all hard to follow the yellow arrows marking the way; they're painted at regular intervals, often within sight of each other, on trees, rocks, sidewalks, fences, the sides of buildings. For the next month of walking we will rarely be even slightly confused about the route, let alone lost. Upon encountering anyone wearing a backpack and a quizzical expression, the local population cheerfully and forcefully directs that peregrino along the path toward the next refugio. Indeed, the difficulty is not staying on the path; it's convincing people that you're looking for anyplace that's *off* the path.

On our way to Zubiri, our first destination, we pass through tidy Basque villages with narrow streets and Alpine-style houses, copses of trees, and pastures with ancient rusting tractors, flocks of sheep, and cows with mournful bells. In a few places we sink up to our boot tops in rich mud, the last we'll see in four hundred miles of dry weather. By this time, we're largely past the temporary disorientation of jet lag and are well into the more durable perplexity of culture shock. We still have a couple of days before the pain starts. It's an easy time. We love being peregrinos.

We spend most of our first day walking by ourselves out of sight of any other pilgrims. This will prove to be the pattern throughout the journey: peregrinos may begin the day in a cluster, but people walk at different speeds and rest at different times and places. Lisa and I will spend most of the next month completely alone with each other.

And yet, we soon discover that peregrinos are pack animals. Beasts of burden, they travel in loosely structured but socially complex herds. Wherever we started from as individuals, a group of us has passed through Roncesvalles at about the same time and so we will reach Santiago within days of each other. The route is the same for all of us, so we only lose track of one another for a few days at most. When someone is having a hard time, the word goes up and down the line and people keep an eye out. When we do meet up, we ask after one another in various languages and provide advice and counsel to one another on places to stay, the treatment of blisters, and so on. There is a sense of fellowship, of people urging one another on. "Ultreya," we say to one another, which, I gather, is a sort of cross between "onward" and "buck up there, pilgrim."

Like dogs (or chickens) it seems important to us to establish a hierarchy. I can sense the competition in the air from the first day, from the first *step* along the path. Unlike other animal groups, the competition for status in our pack doesn't have as much to do with physical strength or sexual selection (though those games are certainly in progress as well) as it does with authenticity. There are some pilgrims here who are more pilgrim than other pilgrims. And some people out here on the Camino aren't *real* pilgrims at all. The bicyclists, for example: everyone who is on foot agrees the bikers aren't real pilgrims, though none of us, as far as I can tell, is ready to start a barroom brawl about it: "Now listen here, *pilgrim*, real pilgrims travel on foot, not wheels."

Actually—though we hikers don't like to admit it—the bicyclists have a certain claim to authenticity. When Franco's government modernized the Spanish roads, parts of the Camino were paved and incorporated into the highway system. Peregrinos who wanted to travel on foot sought alternate footpaths where possible, and these have become the standard modern hiking route. Much of the traditional Way of Saint James is no longer the country lane or the picturesque trail; it's blacktop, and the bikers are right on course.

Then there's the guy doing his pilgrimage on a donkey. He looks like Sancho Panza. What are we supposed to make of him? Where does he fit into the peregrine pecking order? Well, donkeys aren't a modern invention, like, for example, bicycles. Donkeys, at least compared to bicycles, are inconvenient, so that's got to be worth something. Okay, so Sancho isn't part of our pilgrim pack, but we might grant him provisional pilgrim status anyhow. But then, wait a minute: maybe he's trying to outdo us all in terms of being Christlike; maybe he's planning a triumphal entry to the holy city. Sancho and his donkey—who does he think he is? He's friendly enough, but we avoid him.

Within a few days, it seems clear that Lisa and I are also considered provisional members; for one thing, we're the only Americans, which means that—for good or ill—everyone has an *opinion* about us. But mainly we're suspect because we're not staying in the refugios. This proves to be something of a sore spot with us. I find myself running an inner diatribe: *Well, okay, pilgrim. How do you draw the line? What is a real pilgrim anyway, huh? You know, if you were a real pilgrim, you wouldn't just walk to Santiago then fly home. You'd walk back, wouldn't you?*

Then we run into a guy doing exactly that: walking the *other* way on the Camino. He's got a staff, a big cross on a chain around his neck, and he's wearing a black cloak. We stop, turn, and watch him striding resolutely east, upstream against the flow of the herd. He looks more than a little bit crazy. I turn to Lisa and say, "See? Now *there's* a pilgrim."

Then again, who knows? Maybe the whole game is something I am imagining; if anyone has doubts about his authenticity here, it would be me.

Though I can't seem to get rid of this chip on my shoulder, Lisa and I find that we are eager to slough off any physical possessions we can do without. We scan our belongings daily, looking for things to leave behind. Besides my pocket Spanish-English dictionary, I've brought along that phrasebook: redundant. A large ziplock bag of emergency medications: we decide we'll never use them, tra-la.

It's not just a matter of physical weight. We've brought along some (literally) light reading, a couple of paperback novels that together must weigh less than a pound. Usually, books are a solace, a sanctuary in difficult times. But here, after a full day of walking, we find we have no desire to read them. The early stops along the Camino Francés must be littered with such jetsam—over the side they go.

Lisa does love her backpack, though. It serves as a kind of mini-household for her to tidy. It has lots of pockets, you see, and she knows exactly what is in each pocket, large and small. In one pocket, in a little bag with a drawstring, she keeps her chapstick, handiwipes, and lotions. Another contains her water bottle and emergency reserve chocolate bars. In another, a little red notebook and pen are ready to record her observations and impressions. One tiny pocket is devoted to sugar cubes she has collected from bars and restaurants along the way, in case she should meet a friendly horse.

■　　■　　■

On pilgrimage, there is a constant sense of the body in motion, therefore in space, and of the space above and below. For those of us accustomed to spending most of our days indoors, earth and sky regain their significance, and we float free between them. Books, possessions of all kinds, are leaden things, distractions, anchors. Fields of spring wildflowers drift by, poppies by the side of the path, huge purple thistles, sunflowers, gnarled grapevines, olive trees, cow pastures. Ruined castles on the hills. On the high ridges, in the land of Don Quixote, massive wind turbines whoosh and hum. Medieval towns rise in the distance, islands from a sea of cropland. As we approach a town, there is none of the ill-defined transition from country to exurb to suburb to city that has become the norm in the States. The town looms larger, larger, and then we simply arrive, step from fields to town, as we might from a boat to a dock and come upon, in medias res, the life of an insular community.

Most people do not speak to us, the alien beings passing through their lives like neutrinos through the planet. We nod in greeting, and they may nod back, just the slightest motion of the head, but often they, especially the older men in gray cloth caps, simply stare. We are not unwelcome; we are just unrecognizable as individuals, undifferentiated from the parade of strangers that has passed through these streets for a thousand years.

The entire length of the Camino is impossibly layered with history, myth, legend, rumor, literary reference, local tradition, and religious anecdote. Story upon story in an absurd, indigestible Dagwood sandwich of narrative. Our guidebook attempts bite-sized summaries. At first, I try to keep track of it all, reading aloud to Lisa with all the reverence I can muster. Each time we pause to rest at some landmark, I once again whip out the guidebook. Ignoring my fellow traveler's sour expression, I press on valiantly; but I soon find it's impossible to keep a note of helium-high hysteria from creeping into my voice. This rock is famous for being the same length as the stride of the great Roland. After fighting off the Saracens, Charlemagne napped here. This is the very street where El Cid did his El Cid thing. This lovely little church is yet another example of late Gothic construction with Moorish influences—another gem of the Camino.

But wait, there's more: In this church, in order to persuade a notorious skeptic of the reality of transubstantiation, the Communion wafer turned into a chunk of bleeding flesh. In this town, in order to save the life of an innocent young man, a roast chicken came back to life and leapt around the table (I am not making this up); to this day, the townspeople keep a hen and rooster in the church in a golden cage. Hark! The rooster's crow! It brings good luck to pilgrims. And so on. Another mile, another miracle.

Over the side goes the guidebook.

■　■　■

In the towns, once the heat of the day has dissipated, people gather in the main square or street for the evening *paseo*: friends walking arm in arm, looking in shop windows and stopping in the bars for tapas; young couples courting, strolling just beyond the range of their parents' hearing; families visiting with one another; old men playing cards—with a defiant flourish, one of them slaps down the winning card—and the old women in black sitting all on one bench, corvine, watchful. The middle-aged women sit at café tables, smoking, drinking tiny cups of espresso, their legs crossed at the ankles, elegantly turned out in tailored suits, low heels, and silk scarves. Small bands of children dart in and out, supervised by no one and everyone. Men coo and make faces at infants in strollers wearing white cotton dresses and ornate lace caps.

A woman stands by one of the children, a boy about six years old; she's not his mother, but reflexively her hand reaches up and caresses the back of his head. Watching from the margins, we see this gesture repeated in one form or another in town squares all the way across Spain, and always, we feel a pang. What must it be to belong here, to be at home in a society that so adores its children?

We are not always ignored. Indeed, there are times when we are forcefully greeted. On a stretch of the path hemmed in by hedges on one side and a steep bank on the other, we encounter a grizzled man with a cane, wearing a black beret, a military ribbon pinned to his suit jacket. He seizes my hand, asks where we are from, and tells us we are very brave—at least I think that's what he's saying. He shakes my hand again, claps me on the shoulder, kisses Lisa on the cheek, wishes us a good journey, gives us some hard candies from his pocket, then marches on his way.

Another time, upon entering a town, a man in his forties starts talking excitedly to me without preamble, gesticulating, as if trying to call my attention to some obvious and urgent problem. As if, for example, my hat is on fire. I try to decipher what he is saying, and I'm having no luck. I smile and nod as if I understand, then ask him, again, sir, please, kindly to talk more slowly, *mas despacio, por favor*, and to be so good as to repeat himself. After a few minutes, an older man walks up to us, as if to join the conversation. He takes the agitated man by the hand, murmurs something to him (I think he promised him ice cream), and leads him away. I realize that I've been trying to converse with the village idiot. Or vice versa.

Lisa knows not a word of Spanish. Each morning, she practices diligently her one phrase, "Una Coca-Cola, por favor," but by midafternoon, it is forgotten. I am in charge of all the transactions of our day. We joke that she is Queen; she does not touch money, ask directions, or arrange for her accommodations. Those sorts of things are taken care of for her by her people. That would be me.

Given the narrow window of time I had to learn Spanish before our departure, I adopted a set of strategies and parameters, limiting my vocabulary to words that might be useful in all the stock travel situations I could envision. With respect to verbs, I resolved that, for the most part, the past would be irrelevant: I would speak in the present tense, resorting to the infinitive of the verb if necessary. In order to avoid learning the future tense, I decided simply to use the compound construction, *vamos a*, "we are going to. . . ." Another efficiency: second-person Spanish verbs and pronouns present a choice between the familiar *tú* and the formal *usted* forms: not wanting to give offense, I opted for the formal and jettisoned the rest. For good measure, I memorized the most polite forms of address.

As a result, I literally do not know how to speak informally to Spaniards. My Spanish conversation style veers between the blurry, barked half-phrases of a two-year-old and the subjunctive circumlocutions of a nineteenth-century diplomat. Lisa takes great pleasure in watching people's faces as I try to communicate some need. At first, they look a little disoriented as I launch into the equivalent of, "Please, esteeméd sirs, I wonder if you might do us the favor of telling us at what hour of the clock you serve the evening repast," but then the shadow of a smile forms at the corner of the mouth. And they answer slowly, carefully, as a parent would to a precocious child.

In my normal life, I'm not fond of making mistakes, but here I make them all day long, entertaining people wherever I go. For example, there's the fruit stand where I march confidently up to the counter and order half a kilo of swans. The young woman pauses for just a moment before, with a little half smile, she starts to put some plums in a paper bag. I have the feeling I've said something wrong. Then I realize. "*Cisnes* are birds, right?" She nods kindly and, handing me the bag, stifles a giggle. Holding up the bag I ask, "If you please, miss, what do you call these?" She tells me the word I'm looking for is *ciruelas*. Not even close.

Still, I am relieved to find that I can generally make myself understood, and that, when I ask a question, I can usually understand the reply. In fact, in one area, I shine: while, in general, my language skills are below the preschool level, I could earn a master's degree in ordering food. I may not be able to carry on a basic conversation, but if you want a menu translated—plums and swans notwithstanding—I'm your man.

Food on the Camino is cheap, plentiful—the special *menú del dia* for pilgrims typically includes two or three courses plus dessert and wine—and heavy on the meat. The Spanish love their ham. All the grocery store windows have at least one whole pig's leg, complete with hoof. In our normal life, Lisa and I drift in and out of various degrees of vegetarianism. That's not an option here. The salads are awful, the bread is cardboard, and the cooked vegetables are thoroughly demoralized. We exist on fruit, ham sandwiches, yogurt, stews, eggs, and huge chunks of roasted animals. I'm in hog heaven. If I thought I could eat this way all the time without turning my arteries to rebar, I would, no question. Further, in my perpetually adrenalized state, I seem to be able to drink as much wine as I like without getting drunk or feeling hung over the next day.

Lisa's not so happy about our peregrino diet—she likes meat now and again, but not every day, and not in these quantities. Further, any serving that still has recognizable animal features attached to it (hooves, claws, lips) tends to give her the whim-whams. In one restaurant, Lisa is glad to hear that trout is on the menu: finally, a respite from red meat. But, of course, it is served whole, its great milky eye staring accusingly up at her. Discreetly, I behead the Queen's dinner and hide the evidence under a napkin. She manages only a forkful or two before pushing her plate away. For the rest of the meal Lisa sips from her water glass and watches me eat. Occasionally, she gives me her impression of the one-eyed, fishy glare. Undaunted, I continue to enjoy my food.

■   ■   ■

Lisa and I operate on a schedule very different from that of your average Spaniard. Like most peregrinos, in order to cover some distance before the heat of the day, we rise before dawn and set out into the deserted streets—we'll get breakfast midmorning when shops and cafés open. By late afternoon, siesta time, we reach our destination. We collapse, and it is the only time of day we are in sync with the traditional Spanish routine. We shower, nap, and by five o'clock are ready for dinner. Bars and restaurants on the Camino accommodate peregrinos by offering the pilgrim menu as a kind of early bird special, but you don't see many locals there. While we're eating dinner and winding down, the Spanish are taking care of the rest of the day's business. By eight o'clock, when we're ready for bed, the Spanish are ready to party. Dinner is at nine or ten o'clock, then who knows?

When do they sleep? It's a mystery to us. Each night, as we lie in bed with plugs in our ears and pillows over our heads, there are lively discussions in the hotel rooms adjoining ours, a motor is revving somewhere, and something exciting is happening on the street. Early in the trip, we are awakened at one o'clock in the morning by, I swear, six-part harmony from the plaza outside our hotel window. Another time, just as we are drifting off to sleep, we hear what sounds like rifle fire, then the boom of a cannon. A marching band strikes up a lively tune. I ask the next day if we are in town for a particular festival. No, it turns out; it's just Wednesday.

Everywhere we go, any time we step indoors, always, all day and night, at full blast: television. *Fútbol*, news, talk shows, game shows, reality shows. I read somewhere that the Spanish watch more television than any other European nation except the British, but I am sure they make up for coming in second by turning up the volume.

The Spanish just seem to live larger than we do. Cigarette smoke is everywhere. There are no guardrails. (Need I say that no one ever asked for my letter of reference from the Abbot?) It reminds me of my childhood, before people wore seatbelts, before the invention of good and bad cholesterol, before warnings on cigarette packs, before childproof caps, before stranger danger. More than once, I find myself standing in a place where any American business or town would put a barrier and a sign: "Warning, stepping off the edge of this precipice may result in injury or death." Surely, people must sue one another in Spain?

We startle easily. Maybe it's because we've reduced our top velocity to about three miles per hour, and our inner life has slowed to match. We are, in every sense, pedestrian. Usually, our waking life outdoors, especially on days when the Camino is a footpath or country lane, is relatively peaceful. Days when the yellow arrows direct us to walk on the shoulder of a highway are more difficult. The traffic roars and rockets. Jolly peregrino bikers, swift and silent as cats, ride up behind us. As they explode by, they bellow: "¡Hasta Luego!" We respond with a kind of strangled squeak.

■   ■   ■

It's not that hard to walk fifteen or sixteen miles in a day. Like raising a child or staying in a marriage, the hard part is doing it again the next day and the day after that. The terrain is not challenging. We are not leaping from rock to rock or wading across swollen rivers. (Nor is it necessary for us—as it was for medieval pilgrims—to dodge brigands or wild animals.) The guidebooks tell you that, after the Pyrenees, the Camino Francés passes over two mountain ranges, but come on, people, these are just *hills*. We are just putting one foot in front of the other, usually on level ground. But any activity done thousands of times per day starts to wear on a body. Any irritation related to walking becomes a serious matter—a pressure on a sensitive part of the foot, a place where a badly sewn seam chafes the skin. Something felt in the morning as a slight tickle can be an open sore by afternoon.

When it comes to pain, like most men, I aspire to great bravery. However, true physical courage is just not my strong suit. The best I can manage is a temporary sham of stoicism, clamping the lid down on a simmering pot of anxious self-pity. If asked what the matter is, I will emit a wisp or two of dispirited complaining. But inside, again and again, I wail: *Oh, the pain! What will become of me?* I become thin-skinned, quarrelsome, and daunted by the simplest tasks. I have put Lisa on notice that growing old with me is likely to be a challenge.

As a yoga teacher and sometime triathlete, not only is Lisa in great shape physically, she has a certain equanimity in the face of physical difficulty. She sometimes gets headaches that I suspect would send me whimpering to a darkened room, but she just carries on as usual. On the whole, Lisa is better at pain, and so, on the Camino, it makes a certain kind of sense that she is given more of it to deal with.

At the start of the trip, Lisa enjoys two days of distress-free walking. After that, literally every step of the way sends bolts of pain shooting up from her heels. We buy every Dr. Scholl's remedy we can lay our hands on, taping Lisa's heels, padding her boots, packing and repacking her feet, all to no avail. It will take us a couple of hundred miles of walking before we come to the conclusion that her boots are *too* well worn—no matter how we cushion them, they just aren't absorbing enough impact—and that we should just buy her some new shoes.

Though Lisa's distress is not my fault, I do somehow feel responsible. A reasonable person, seeing what Lisa is going through, would be concerned, but

I feel profoundly unsettled, as if each unsuccessful remedy is a personal failure of character on my part—for which, of course, I blame Lisa. I've been therapized enough to know that this behavior is neurotic, that I should be able to separate my experience from hers, and that I should let her have her bad experience while I have my not-so-bad experience, blah, blah, blah. Looking for some guidance, I telephone a friend in the States. He says something to the effect of: "Whew! What to do when the woman's unhappy? That's a tough one, buddy. Hey, *vaya con Dios.*" (Oddly, this helps.)

We would do better if we slept more, but cheap hotel rooms (often the only hotel rooms available) take their toll. It's not just the noise. At least half of the hotel beds are outfitted with polyester linens (an oxymoron if ever there was one). Would sleeping in plastic trash bags be worse? Hard to say. Often, we have single beds, but when they give us a queen-sized bed, it is stained, it is littered with pubic hairs of many colors, and it features at its head what we come to refer to as the uni-pillow—a four-foot tube of foam rubber in a long pillowcase, intended to be shared as the bed is shared: with each other, with difficulty, and with all the previous occupants and their effluvia. I'm not particularly squeamish about such things, but after a few nights in cheap hotels, I come to the conclusion that it's best to sleep fully dressed. The lighting of the rooms is uncertain and eccentric. One bed has light switches built into the headboard. As we sit up to write in our journals, we keep inadvertently turning the lights off with our posteriors. Later, just when I've drifted off to sleep, I wake to a glaring light in my eyes; I've turned the switch on with my head.

It's not that we expected walking four hundred miles to be easy, but somehow this level of physical and emotional difficulty has taken us by surprise. By now, it has crossed our minds that we might not be able to make it the whole way. The Pilgrim's Blessing—the one we found it so hard to take seriously at the start of the journey—may not be as hyperbolic as we had assumed. All along the Camino there are reminders that this journey was once considered perilous. Indeed, some of the monuments to fallen pilgrims are of recent vintage, though modern fatalities along the Way of Saint James tend to be the result of road accidents rather than wolf packs.

Dying en route was not the worst calamity a medieval pilgrim could suffer. To the faithful, dying on pilgrimage was a shortcut: those who did were said to have attained the same release from purgatory as those who actually completed the journey. But the prospect of remaining alive while somehow being prevented from reaching Santiago so terrified pilgrims that a tradition arose whereby those who were too ill to make it over the final mountain range into Galicia could obtain absolution by passing through the side entrance of the church at Villafranca del Bierzo, what became known as the "Door of Pardon."

While neither of us believes in purgatory, by now we have much at stake in completing this journey. The notion that we might have to quit, hang up the scallop shell and go home, embarasses us. It's one thing to choose an unusual path, to risk being labeled an eccentric. (When we told our friends what we were doing, they said: "You're going to *walk*? They don't have cars in Spain?") It's quite another to return from your path, like Quixote, a *failed* eccentric. More importantly, the prospect of failure dismays us because, whatever the state of our religious convictions, completing this pilgrimage has come to mean more to us than a simple investment of time and money. It is our basic training, our boot camp. This trip is about our future together, and now it feels like our lives are on the line.

We are not quite halfway there.

3.

Our twelfth day on the Camino, we rise before dawn and set off into windy starless darkness. Our destination is the cathedral city of Burgos, eighteen miles away. The uphill path is steep, and Lisa isn't feeling well. By the time we reach a place where the path levels off, passing through straight rows of planted pine forest on a red dirt road, she has already vomited several times. We pass a monument "To the Fallen"—which fallen, it's hard to make out.

By early afternoon, I figure we are within five miles of the city, but Lisa is weak and gray-faced. We arrive in the main square of a small town, and she sinks down to rest on the front steps of a house and take a few sips from her water bottle. Under any other circumstance it would be clear to us what to do next. (Should Lisa find the quickest way to go directly to bed? Or should we go for a spirited five-mile hike? Hmm.) At this point, however, we are so invested in walking that considering any faster and less-strenuous form of transportation has become an existential crisis. We walk, therefore we are. What happens if we stop walking?

Lisa begins to retch. She can't even keep the water down. A man walks up to us—as it turns out, it's his front stoop my wife is puking on. I ask him please would he be so kind as to telephone for a taxi.

Riding to Burgos, it is as though we have been seized in the talons of an enormous raptor and are being transported in one breathtaking swoop from the countryside to the city. Five miles in a terrifying blur, and we are deposited on the steps of the Hotel Norte y Londres. Our room on the top floor is lovely, quiet, clean, and cool, with chenille bedspreads, hardwood floors, and a claw-foot bathtub under the dormer windows. Lisa lies down to rest, but sleep won't come and the dry heaves continue. I go back downstairs and ask the hotel clerk to call for another taxi.

Negotiating Lisa's admission to the Hospital General Yagüe presents certain challenges. First, no one speaks English, so the intake interview involves a great deal of gesturing and frantic flipping through my little pocket dictionary. This is not one of the standard travel situations for which I have prepared. The doctor asks: is Lisa *embarazada*? Somehow, I remember that the word does not mean "embarrassed"—he's asking if she's pregnant. Pause. Lisa and I look at each other, and she bursts into tears. Could be, I tell the doctor, but we don't think so.

Other symptoms besides the vomiting? No. Has she eaten or drunk something unusual? Well, yes, but as far as we know, I have consumed everything she has, and I feel fine. The doctor explains that since Lisa's stomach has been irritated by something to the point where it will not tolerate even water, then she must be admitted to the hospital and hydrated intravenously—a complicated idea, and it takes a while before I can understand what he's trying to get across. He tells us that Lisa will need to stay overnight.

I am reassured, but Lisa is anything but. It's not just that she is ill, has been in constant pain for ten days, and is completely unable to communicate directly with the people who can help her; it's that Lisa is terrified of hospitals. In a sense, the problem is that her health has always been exceptional: she has been spared the kind of childhood accidents I took for granted as if they were standard issue. I've been knocked unconscious a couple of times, broken a bone in my arm, and had other reasons to visit the emergency room. I hate hospitals same as anyone else, but any time I've been to one—or visited someone else in one—things have always turned out fine. In the Mayberry R.F.D. of my mind, doctors are your friends and hospitals are places where you go to get better. To date, Lisa's experience of hospitals is that they are places where friends and relatives go when they are very, very sick, and then they die.

So when we learn that I will not be allowed to stay with Lisa—that after visiting hours I will have to leave the building—it takes a while to gently peel her off me. The emergency room is busy, not inner-city frantic, but there are other people here who are urgently in need of care. As such, the staff has been remarkably thorough and patient with us, making absolutely sure that we have told them any relevant information and that we understand what needs to happen now. I can see, however, that we are beginning to test their tolerance. Yes, Lisa will need to be admitted to the hospital. No, we don't know why she's ill. Yes, she'll be fine. They stop short of rolling their eyes, but it's clear they've had enough of the tourist with the tummy ache.

I settle my sobbing wife in a crisp hospital bed in a room—reassuringly—right next to the nurses' station. They hook her up to an IV tube; Lisa is terribly thirsty, but the doctor has said that for the time being she should not have even small sips of water. The nurse brings her a paper cup with a single ice cube. Soon, it's time for me to go.

When I come to collect Lisa the next morning, she looks and feels much better. She's sitting up in bed and warily regarding the hospital breakfast in front of her. She hasn't had much sleep. All night long, gales of laughter and clouds of cigarette smoke have come billowing from the nurses' station. Now and then, a nurse would come to check on her and bring her another ice cube. The nurses seemed sympathetic when they were in the room, but afterward Lisa could hear them next door: "Chat chat chat *peregrina* chat chat chat chat chat *boo hoo hoooo*." Then more laughter.

When it seems as though Lisa will be able to keep down a few bites of Jell-O and scrambled eggs, we're out of there. Another taxi back to the hotel, and with Lisa once more ensconced in our room, I reconnoiter, scouting for provisions: bottled water, instant sports-drink mixes to replace lost electrolytes, flowers, soaps, lotions, and soft, bland, pale food. In the grocery store, I am the only male; at the checkout counter, the women coo at me and usher me to the front of the line. When I return to the hotel room, Lisa is asleep. Over the next twenty-four hours, she will get out of bed for brief periods but then quickly fall back to sleep wherever she happens to be: in a chair, in the tub, and, after a couple of minutes of yoga, on the floor.

For the next two days, we hole up in the room, and as Lisa's stomach recovers, I fetch slightly more colorful and flavorful food. Lisa tells me she feels like a baby bird. It's humiliating: here she thought she'd have a jaunty little trip and write a jaunty little article about it for the yoga studio newsletter. But now, she's just another dirty pilgrim with vomit on her shoes.

■   ■   ■

We start to make shaky trips together to see some of what the town has to offer. We still don't know (and we never do find out) what made Lisa ill, and now I've started to feel a little nauseated myself. Perhaps it's the easing of stress as Lisa recovers—I feel a little ill because now I can—or maybe it's just flat-out hypochondria: the inability to distinguish her troubles from mine, writ large. Passing through a portico with Jesus at the center and his apostles arrayed around him, we stumble into the cathedral and collapse in a pew, stunned in the cool dimness, staring up at the oceans of cool glass as if from the sandy bottom. Some of the gothic arches are topped not with the wan angular faces of saints, but with more florid folk, all manner of expressions on their faces; now and again, at random intervals, a demon! A tourist pamphlet speculates that the proletarian faces are portraits of the builders—stone masons' caricatures of one another. It goes on to say that this building was started in the thirteenth century, and the first phase of construction took about forty years. Then there was a little problem with funding and, what with the Black Death killing off a third of the population of Europe, a two-hundred-year construction delay. Then another hundred years of construction and the building was completed in the mid-sixteenth century—it took only about seventeen generations.

In such a world, did people even *have* deadlines? What must it have been like to work with the most basic of hand tools, chipping away at something that will not be completed in your great-grandson's lifetime? I cannot imagine. In my workplace, we deal in timelines of three-month semesters, a fiscal year or two at most; developing a ten-year plan is regarded as visionary. Like Everyman, however much I try to expand my perspective to see life in a wider context, I find myself drawn inexorably back to the myopia of trying to achieve the goal in front of me, as if there were no life beyond this project. As if there were no death.

And here, now, on the Camino, despite all the soaring stone evidence before us, Lisa and I can't think in such grand terms for more than a passing moment; we're having a hard time figuring out what we're going to do about the next couple of weeks. We've got to get back to Seattle, and each unscheduled day of rest decreases our margin for completing the trip within the time allotted.

We decide to skip about forty miles of the Camino, to take the bus and resume our walk from Frómista, two stops down the line of our itinerary. And though it feels like cheating, we console ourselves that we'd be eligible for a Compostela even if we started in Sarria and only walked the last sixty miles to Santiago. As we're inquiring at the front desk about public transportation, there's a guy in the back who says he'll drive us this afternoon.

Miguel is a painter and an actor, and he's enthusiastic in his talking and his driving, both of which he does at great speed. When he finds out I'm a theater professor, he has a lot to tell me about Art and Life. In our brief time together in this metal box hurtling down the arrow-straight highway, I catch maybe a third of what he's saying. As a fellow artist, he regards me as a comrade in arms, and he's a little put off by my formal manner of speaking. I try to tell him that it's not personal, that it's just my baby Spanish, but when you only speak baby Spanish, it's hard to explain why you only speak baby Spanish.

West of Burgos, the plains begin. The Tableland, the Meseta: one hundred miles of wheat fields, all the way to León. Before Burgos, the terrain Lisa and I hiked through included woodlands, rolling hills, and rich river-valley bottom-land, but now, abruptly, the landscape is a different story altogether, as if we've been reading a book, and we've skipped an important chapter. In every direction, as far as we can see, besides the road itself and the path beside it, there's nothing but wheat. There's a gravel path running parallel to us about ten yards to our right. But for the grace of Miguel, that's where we would be walking. About three miles short of the town of Frómista, in what seems like, literally, the middle of nowhere, we ask Miguel to let us out. "¿Aqui?" he asks, and it's a good question.

We explain to Miguel that we're going to walk the rest of the way to town, just to get the feel of it again. He smiles and shrugs. "Buen Camino," he says. We get out of the car, and at that very moment some pilgrims walk by (where did they come from?). With a spray of gravel, Miguel does a quick U-turn and is gone. We nod at the pilgrims, acting casual, and they give us a *look*: What, not only do you stay in hotels, now you're *hitching*?

.　　.　　.

We begin walking again. The three miles to Frómista are utterly featureless—a preview of coming attractions. From here, each day, all day, until León, we are on the plains, the plains, the plains. Each morning: Wheat. Blue sky. Sun rising behind us. Gravel path. Our shadows in front of us. Wheat. Walking. Highway shoulder. Pavement. Yellow arrow. Heat shimmer. Horizon. Stand of poplars. Sun overhead. Earth turning. Wheat. Sky. Truck. Another mile. BIKER! Pause.

Breathe. Walking. Sky. Sun in front of us now. Bug. Wheat. Still on the plains. Another day: tedium, rinse, repeat.

And the rain in Spain? Let me tell you something, Professor Higgins: the plain may be the one place in Spain that, mainly, it does not rain. On the map you can see blue lines indicating rivers, but when we cross them they turn out to be neither rivers nor streams but dry drainage ditches. The blue dots on the map are neither lakes nor ponds; they are puddles.

This is the time of the blisters: we've had some before, but now we get them in abundance. They are fruitful and multiply: on toes, on heels, on the soles, on the tops of our feet. Clear blisters, blood blisters, blisters inside of blisters. Blisters under calluses, blisters under toenails—I lose the nail on my little toe. This is not exceptional, just ordinary suffering, peregrino business as usual. Lisa, however, doesn't just get the standard-issue peregrina blisters: at one point, almost the entire sole of her right foot *is* a blister.

A large part of our limited social life consists of discussing (as far as language and gesture allow) the advantages and disadvantages of particular footwear. We stand by our boots; they are comfortable and well worn in, we maintain; they provide good protection and ankle support, and look: we've got special socks designed to wick perspiration away. Still, we have to admit that even in the best boots, heat and moisture can build up creating the ideal nurturing environment for blisters. Some pilgrims opt for sandals. Solves the ventilation problem, but I don't know: fifteen, twenty miles a day on sandals? We allow there's a possibility that running shoes might be worth a try, especially for walking on pavement. However, it will be a few days' walk until we are in a town of a size large enough to contain a shoe store, so the point is moot. In the meantime, we get all kinds of advice about the blisters. Leave them be. Put moleskin around them. Drain them. Grease them. Cover them. Don't.

We try every remedy offered and settle on the most seemingly bizarre: what you do is you thread a needle, cut the thread very short, dip it in alcohol. Then you push the needle in one side of your blister and pull it out the other, leaving a small amount of thread hanging from both sides of the blister. You cut the thread and you leave it that way all night, letting the thread wick the moisture out of the blister. Each night, Lisa and I sit side by side, sewing toes. Each morning, we remove the threads from the desiccated blisters and spend half an hour rebandaging and padding our feet for the day.

Then it's time for the sunscreen ritual. It takes Lisa only a couple of minutes to dab some on to her rapidly bronzing arms and legs. I am another story. I do not tan. At my darkest, I am beige, and that's that, except for the pink parts. Nothing on me that is beige or pink will ever become brown. So, every morning, I slather my body with sunblock from my ankles to the top of my head. Whitey Starts His Day. I pay particular attention to the left side of my body; when you're always walking due west, that's the side of the body with southern exposure. Of course, I do have one advantage over my wife: I don't have to put on a sports bra. As Lisa says, there's really nothing like a clammy sports bra at six A.M.

In some sections of the path, volunteers have planted shade trees. In thirty years or so, these trees will provide comfort for hot and weary peregrinos. At this particular moment in history, however, mile after mile, they are merely sticks.

We are ants marching across a skillet. The only physical relief from the heat comes when we pass through a dusty town and scuttle into a hole-in-the-wall bar. "Una Coca-Cola, por favor."

Fortunately, at day's end, every hotel we stay in on this leg of the journey is relatively quiet and clean. At the moment, we're not picky; just being indoors feels like a luxury, but some of these places are real oases, isolated and lush. At the Hotel San Zoilo, a former monastery, our room looks out over the cloisters and a symmetrical garden with a fountain at its center. Peacocks wander about; now and then, one of them jumps onto the lower limb of a tree, looks surprised and anxious that he's actually arrived there, and sounds his barbaric yawp. In response, from their huge nest on top of the clock tower—whose iron hands indicate a perpetual six o'clock—three storks clack their bills. We roam the building, checking out the tapestries and carvings, the dusty, disused chapel. It is as if we have been locked in a museum after closing time.

In one of the hallways, we find a series of openings in the wall, each niche about two feet square at the entrance and extending back about eight or ten feet into darkness. We ask the concierge at the front desk, who looks puzzled. Holes? We describe them and tell her our guesses. Were they storage spaces? Ovens? Tombs? Ah, she says, the holes in the wall you refer to were used as punishment cells. When a monk believed he had done something sinful, he would isolate himself for a time in one of these stone coffins. She takes a drag on her cigarette and cocks an eyebrow at us: "Sinful. Now what do you suppose a monk could have gotten up to way out here?"

4.

For lack of other material on the plains, my journal of the trip mostly chronicles our various physical injuries and marital spats. In a sense, without anything else to keep track of, I am keeping score, not so much of who wins our daily rows, but of how quickly we're able to move through them. Early in our marriage, we would have luxuriant fights that lasted for days. Now, who needs it? We aim for efficiency.

It's not hard to see why we're fighting. For the first time since she was a child, Lisa is completely dependent. She has no conversation with anyone but me, no way to meet her needs except through me. When I am balky, reluctant to negotiate some obstacle, can't figure out the words, she's out of luck. Most of the time, I come through. When I don't, she feels panicky and helpless, and I feel put upon. She snipes; I bully. The routine becomes so familiar that, at one point, we go through it from start to finish, from sarcasm to squabble to sulking to tearful reconciliation in twenty minutes flat.

If we were to reduce it even further, the script might read as follows:

> HER: Why don't you help me?
> ME: I will. You need to trust me.

HER: You need to earn that trust.
ME: Trust me, and I'll step up.
HER: Step up, and I'll trust you.
ME: Bark.
HER: Waaah.

Later, in our hotel room, we take off our filthy socks, put them on our hands, and do a reprise of our fight in gibberish starring the Sock Puppet Peregrinos. This is the highlight of our day.

Without such cheap thrills, amusement would be in short supply here on the Meseta. We've managed to acquire a paperback murder mystery in English, so we're doing a little reading in the evenings. As we have only the one book, and we're too tired to read aloud to one another, Lisa reads a chapter, and when she's done with it, she rips it out of the book so that I can read it as she continues on with the next chapter. When I'm done with it, I put the chapter in the trash. Absurdly, having lightened our load by perhaps an ounce, I feel virtuous every time I do this.

But the evenings aren't the hard part; the sheer punishing bleary sameness of each day, of each hour, walking through these fields is the hard part. Through the heat haze, we see the red flecks of poppies among the wheat stalks; Lisa and I speculate that Spanish bread is psychotropic—that, along with the espresso, explains a lot about the Spanish. Perhaps it is having its effect on me as well. I start doing little math problems in my head. If the higher estimates are right, around the year 1200, nearly 3.4 percent of Europe's population traveled to Santiago per year. That can't be. At that rate, it would mean that—not counting those who did the pilgrimage more than once—the entire population of Europe, every single person, every infant, every octagenarian, would have visited Santiago within thirty years. Two million peregrinos per year would be an average of 5,500 per day arriving in Santiago. A pilgrim every sixteen seconds. Had they all walked the Camino Francés, that would have meant an average of one pilgrim every five yards. Not close enough together to form a single conga line, but then—as I recall—it would be many years before the conga became an international sensation.

So much for math. "Oh, look," I say to Lisa, "there's some wheat."

The brain in pain is mainly on the plain. Telling the brain to imagine arriving at our destination just makes it worse. We're not there. No, we're here. And it's hot.

In unpleasant situations, I turn to humor. In general, it's a strength, but my mordant sense of humor does sometimes get me into trouble. One time, when I was in my teens, a girl I was trying to impress told me that her dog had had a litter the night before, but it was unseasonably cold; several of the pups had frozen to death. "Pupsicles!" I blurted. She never spoke to me again.

On the Camino, mordant humor does not help. When I remark to Lisa that we put the grim in pilgrim, she doesn't even crack a smile. I make jokes about fried pilgrim, plank-roasted pilgrim, pilgrim flambé, and so on. Lisa tells me to shut my piehole—such remarks just make the burning worse. She's right; I shut up. Then Lisa has a better idea: pilgrim sorbet, pilgrim frappé. We design a full cool pilgrim *menú del dia*: pilgrims au naturel on a bed of moss, pilgrim gazpacho, pilgrim glacé, pilgrim cocktail (shaken not stirred), peregrino popsicles. That's better.

For a while.

Wheat. Sky. Truck. Heat shimmer.

What to do? Back in the States, when we were planning this, we said we'd pray. Now would be a good time, wouldn't it? Maybe to James?

Alright, deep breath. I picture James in my mind. All along the route, we have seen statues of him, not as he might have looked in the time of Christ, but dressed as a medieval pilgrim. When I first see this, my literal mind balks: it's like looking at a portrait of Jesus in chinos and an oxford shirt. But I remind myself that the sense of time here is different, Everyman's time, God's time: all time and no time at all. The people who carved these images weren't interested in showing the James who had died in the first century, but the James who is present, the patron and protector of pilgrims here and now. They show him serene-faced, a gentle presence, a reminder of journey's end, and a figure of enduring benediction.

And then there are the depictions of James not as a pilgrim but as the patron saint of Spain, a warrior on a horse. In the earliest days of the pilgrimage, most of the southern part of the Iberian peninsula was still under Moorish rule. Of necessity, pilgrims coming by land took this northern route through a narrow ribbon of Christian territory defended by the Knights Templar. The establishment of the Camino de Santiago worked in tandem with—and indeed was a means of—driving the Moors from the peninsula and uniting the various Christian kingdoms into what we now know as Spain. Just as Lisa and I have started to get used to the image of James the mild peregrino, we find we also have to come to terms with the image of him killing black people with a spear. I make a quiet decision: at least for the present, I'm going to keep in mind the fierceness of the image rather than its violence. Determination we could use. But hold the genocide, please.

Is *this* prayer—keeping these images in mind? It helps a little, I notice. I kind of like hanging out with the Jameses in my head. But should I be talking to them?

How to pray? Some Buddhists practice walking meditation in which they try to bring mindfulness to each step. My mother, who lives near a New-Age retreat center in upstate New York, once called me up and told me she had just seen the darndest thing: a whole field full of people staring at the ground and walking in slow motion. Did I know anything about this? Was this the latest thing? Was it some kind of prank?

On this trip, we had intended to practice a kind of walking meditation— though at regular speed and with a destination—trying to stay in the present moment, really notice what is going on around us, truly experience every step of the way. Pain is a not-so-gentle reminder of every step of the way. This step hurts! And so does this one! And this one too! In this sense, we are both very much in the present, thank you, though this was not the present we had in mind.

So here I am back at the old question of how to pray in words. Lisa and I had discussed trying out different varieties of prayer: prayers of praise, prayers of thanks, prayers of compassion. Instead, uncomfortable, irritable, and worried, I grab the plastic telephone in my head and start barking the same prayer over and over again into the receiver: help.

Of course, I realize that part of my problem with praying is that I have no idea whether God exists. This issue notwithstanding, I decide to stick with it, but after a couple of hours of asking Whoever Might Be Listening to please, please fix this for me, I feel worse. It's as if I'm in the back seat asking God every five minutes: *Are we there yet?*

A therapist I know is fond of saying that whining is just anger through a small hole. Realizing that I am indeed angry, I consider opening up the hole a bit, trying an angry prayer. I'm thinking that raging at God would at least be more genuine than whining. But this trip isn't God's fault; we're not doing this under duress. This is not the Bataan Death March; we're here by choice. So maybe, I say to myself, you should quit praying for God to swoop down, part the sea of wheat, and deliver you to the other side. Maybe you should pray for God to help you find the strength, the courage, and the good judgment *in yourself* to complete this pilgrimage, and to see to Lisa's needs when she can't fend for herself. What's needed here is agency, not victimhood. God is not the problem;

you are the problem. Grow up, for Christ's sake. And put down that stupid toy phone, will you?

As soon as I pray this way, if this is praying, I feel better. Not just emotionally but physically: suddenly, the pain is gone. I know, it's not much of a miracle; I wasn't filled with blue light; warmth did not radiate from my heart chakra and suffuse my limbs with a tingly sense of well-being. Still, my whole life, I've never experienced anything like it before: prayer as analgesic. I stop walking for a moment and stand there grinning like an idiot. *Wait*, I say. *Do that again.*

.   .   .

Dusk. We are still three days' walk from the far edge of the Meseta. Now we can see the mountains in the distance. As we approach today's destination, Burgo Ranero, my brain strikes up a game of "Translate That Town"—something I've been doing since the start of the trip. I do realize that, with my baby Spanish and my ignorance of history, my translations are suspect. After all, if I were a Spaniard walking across the United States, how would I translate "Pittsburgh"? Holesville? But this doesn't deter my brain. *Burgo* is town. *Ranero?* The Spanish word for frog is *rana*—I know this from my graduate-level work in menu studies (though we have yet to encounter frogs' legs in any bar or restaurant along the way, I am prepared). So: Frogtown? Or, since a *ranchero* is a rancher, a *ranero* would be a frogger, right? "Froggerville, just like I pictured it," I announce to Lisa. But I don't see any frogs. How could there be frogs? There's no *water* here.

Suddenly the sky fills with thunderclouds. Where did they come from? We step inside our hotel lobby just as they open up. Sheets of rain splash against the windows; it is as if we are on the bridge of a ship in a low-budget movie set and the film crew is trying to simulate a typhoon by throwing buckets of water. By the time we're settled in our room, the storm is over. Rain? What rain?

Next morning, we leave Burgo Ranero in the cool dark. Today's walk to León will be our longest so far, nearly twenty-two miles. Clear sky, stars overhead; no doubt, it will be just as hot as yesterday and the day before. Our departure doesn't set off the usual cacophony of barking dogs. Instead, at the far end of town, where there is a large puddle the sanguine Froggervillians call a lake, a chorus of frogs gives us a rousing send-off. They sing a kind of acid jazz, as if they are being played backward. One last hallucinogenic day on the plains.

By midmorning, we're dripping sweat, and I'm having frequent, epic sneezing fits—some new allergen lurks in the wheat fields. By midafternoon, it's clear to us that we're going to have to find a way to wait out the worst of the heat, and if I don't get myself and my sinuses inside, I fear that I will explode in a fine pink mist. A motel emerges from the heat shimmer. We check in, shower, and lie down with cool washcloths across our eyes. We wake up refreshed and make love.

It's still blazing hot out. We consider spending the night, but we've planned a rest day in a five-star hotel in León; it'd be a shame to spend it on the plains instead. And we feel positively chipper after our midday tryst. (*Ultreya?* You betcha.) We decide to check out of the hotel and press on. I'm prepared to offer the man at the desk an explanation—I don't want him to think we weren't happy with his motel—but he takes back the key and accepts payment for the room without question. A couple checking in for a couple of hours then leaving with that just-got-laid glow? Apparently this is not unusual at his motel. There is a rack of yellowing postcards on the counter, showing the motel surrounded by seventies-era automobiles. I buy one as a keepsake.

We aren't far from our no-tell motel before I start to wonder if maybe we should have stayed there. It's brutally hot, and my feet are more than usually blistered. Trying to keep the pressure off the blisters alters my stride, slightly at first, but significantly: here come the salad forks. By the time we reach the river Bernesga (a real river at last), on the outskirts of León, I'm limping like something out of a horror movie. Eyes on the prize, zombie. Still more than a mile to go.

Now on city streets, the Camino continues along the riverbank. We are in the home stretch when Lisa, love of my life—as she does, I swear, whenever we are nearing our destination—*slows down*. (It does not occur to me that I may have unconsciously sped up.) For a while, I try to rein myself in and stay with her, but eventually I can't stand it anymore. I stagger at full speed leaving her behind. I may be a lame horse, but I am nearing the barn.

And not just any barn. The hotel we rough beasts are slouching toward is a *parador*, one of a chain of state-run hotels founded in 1928 by King Alfonso XIII just before he was deposed. Alfonso's reign began well enough. When he came of age and assumed the throne in 1902, the country held a week-long fiesta, with bullfights, dances, and parades. A reporter for a French newspaper called the young king "the happiest and best loved of all the rulers of the earth." Then Alfonso lost Cuba, Puerto Rico, the Philippines, and nearly lost Spanish Morocco. In response to a constant stream of withering disparagement from the Spanish parliament, Alfonso stood by while the military established a dictatorship under the brutal Miguel Primo de Rivera whom the king blithely dubbed his prime minister. Alfonso then abandoned statecraft for hostelry (he had taken an interest in hotels after he was unable to house all the guests for his wedding), a profession for which he was much more suited, establishing profitable first-class hotels all across Spain in fortresses, castles, palaces, manor houses, convents, monasteries, and other historic structures. I suppose every fascist has his sunny side. Hitler liked dogs. Mussolini, it is said, made the trains run on time. Alfonso, well, he put mints on the pillows.

The phrase "government-run hotel chain" does not sound promising to an American; it conjures a vision of prefabricated, cracker-box housing projects, soap shortages, early curfews, meals of surplus cheese. To say that a five-star Spanish parador is merely the antithesis of this vision would be an understatement. A five-star Spanish parador is about as close as real life gets to Coleridge's pipe dream of Xanadu.

When I reach the Plaza de San Marcos, I stop to wait for Lisa to catch up. For a moment, we stare across the square at the great white stone facade of the Hotel San Marcos, a hundred yards across, ornately carved with religious and historical scenes. This is some place, folks; and we—as we near the entrance with our sweat-stained backpacks, our dangling socks, our weathered faces, and our chronic foot ailments—we are the Clampetts. Howdy.

The clerk finds our reservation and gestures grandly to a bellhop in a pristine uniform who, despite our embarrassed protests, shoulders both of our filthy backpacks and heads for the elevator. He shows us to our room and, with some effort, manages to perch our packs on the luggage stand. I retrieve a couple of limp bills from the travel wallet I wear on a cord around my neck, and as I hand them to him I say: Where were you twenty miles ago? He smiles politely, acknowledging the joke, then slips out of the room, silently closing the door after him. For a moment we just stand there in the middle of the oriental carpet, stunned, our hands and arms pulled in, as if we might ruin anything we touch.

Actually, given the state of our personal hygiene, ruining things by touching them is a real possibility. First order of business: self-fumigation. We strip and head for the bathroom.

We wash our clothes and ourselves twice over, pilgrim-style. On the Way of Saint James, Laundromats being few and far between, what you do is soak your clothes in the sink with a little laundry soap. Then you get in the shower along with your clothes, trampling them underfoot like the grapes of wrath as you soap and rinse your body. You wring out the clothes, dry yourself, then roll up the clothes in the towel and jump up and down on the roll. Your clothes may not exactly be clean, but for the peregrino, after a certain point in the journey, cleanliness becomes more of an Edenic abstraction rather than a physically attainable state. You hang your clothes up to dry, and whatever items are still damp the next morning you attach to the back of your pack, hoping the morning air and sun will dry them before you are seen actually parading your dirty laundry through town. Tonight, we're aiming for a higher standard of cleanliness than usual: we'd very much like to go to dinner here in the parador without stinking up the dining room.

The original building on this site was a monastery, with a church and hospital attached, founded in the twelfth century to take care of filthy, ailing, and otherwise bedraggled pilgrims—back then, we'd have fit right in. But then, in the sixteenth century, the monastery was rebuilt on a grander scale and began to attract a wealthier clientele. Cloisters, a church, and a palatial tower were added in the seventeenth and eighteenth centuries. The minibar is late twentieth, perhaps early twenty-first century.

Double brandy in hand, I perch on the sink and soak my feet in the bidet as Lisa luxuriates in the massive marble tub. If we ever do this again, says Lisa, it's paradors all the way, baby. I pad back to the bedroom and am greeted by a familiar reek: our packs are beyond hope—I toss them in the closet and shut the door.

Our room looks out over the narrow river and a stone bridge. We've thrown open the windows to let in the soft early evening air. As we wait for our clothes to dry and the sores on our feet to scab over, we sit naked side by side on the king-sized bed, writing in our journals. Strings of lights twinkle in the trees on the opposite bank of the river, and we can see couples strolling on the promenade. Somewhere just out of sight, a flute and guitar: street musicians playing Bach. Lisa puts her notebook aside and, like an explorer thanking God for dry land, she lies face down on the bed, running her hands over the crisp, cool linens. "Can you *believe* this?" she asks me. "What do you suppose the *thread count* is on these sheets?"

■　　■　　■

At this point in the trip, Lisa's letters home get positively chirpy, as if someone has removed the cover from her birdcage. Of our room, she writes, "This is the most swell place I've EVER been!"

On our way to dinner, we hobble through some of the public rooms, the lobbies, hallways, and lounges: room after room of lush carpets, huge dark oil paintings, tapestries, white marble, and bronze statuary. At the entrance to the cavernous dining room, as we wait for the maître d' to seat us, we are relieved to see that the diners are not nearly as elegant as we had feared. Were the room full of Spaniards, we would appear shabby indeed. Instead, it's full of tourists in their finest synthetic wrinkle-free fabrics. They're better dressed and cleaner than we are, but elegant? Hardly.

The menu is in three languages, left to right, Spanish, French, English. Among the appetizers: "Ancas de Rana." Scan to the right: "Cuisses de Grenouilles, Legs of Frogs." What do you know? I mutter a quick prayer that they aren't the ones who were singing to us this morning, and to be on the safe side, I order the "Mousse of Pippers" instead. The dessert section includes something called "Cheery Cream."

This isn't a place for pilgrims. Lisa continues to chirp, but I can feel my mood sinking and my conversation degenerates to intermittent grunts. The food is decent and plentiful, but it seems somehow insubstantial compared to what we've gotten used to in our peregrino dives. It's oddly quiet. People mumble to one another at their various tables. Little islands. I take an immediate dislike to the tourists at the next table. Feeding their pale fat larval children, they disgust me. I disgust me. I overeat, and I drink too much.

I realize that I'm engaged in a strenuous feat of mental gymnastics, projecting the qualities I dislike in myself onto those around me and blaming them for my own shortcomings. I know there's nothing wrong with the people at the next table over. They're probably perfectly nice well-fed, pale, northern Europeans attired in their various pastel shades of polyester. And yet I can't stop myself. The Beatles' song "Piggies" plays merrily on an endless loop in my head as I shovel hearty spoonfuls of cheery cream into my mouth.

I have recurrent episodes of this sort of emotional seizure throughout our stay at the parador, which we decide to extend a day longer. Most of the time, I'm just fine and glad not to be walking. Sometimes I am lucid enough to actually be grateful that Lisa and I have the time and the money to do what we're doing. I like luxury, who doesn't? But when I'm in the middle of such abundance, I am like the child of overindulgent parents, surrounded by birthday gifts, ripping open box after box, no longer aware of the contents, just desperate for more.

Lisa doesn't seem to have any of these problems. Luxury suits her. She enjoys being pampered. She appreciates quality. She rarely overindulges in anything. When it's time to work, she works, and when it's time to rest, she rests.

How on earth do we stand one another? Trying to work things out in my journal, I wonder at some length whether each of us thrives on the other's misery. What if our marriage is a zero-sum game? Once again, looking for some guidance, I telephone my friend back home. "So what should I do when the woman's happy and *I'm* the one who's depressed?" He tells me I'm going to have to suck it up and enjoy the hotel.

■ ■ ■

That afternoon, after a visit to the Cathedral, we sit in the park eating ham sandwiches under a canopy of shade trees. Once again, an idyllic scene, but I can feel myself sinking into the sedative ooze. Lisa tries to draw me out, but all she receives are brief reports from the interior: *Agree sandwiches very good* STOP. *Trees nice* STOP. END OF MESSAGE.

At such times I am my father. Normally an easygoing man with an infectious laugh, a man who delighted in people's eccentricities and would often tell me funny stories about the ones he'd run across during his workday, my father would at times sink far into himself. He was never cold, but like many men of his generation, he was often blank. A skilled business negotiator, weak hand or strong, he played his cards close to the chest. I suspect that he struggled with depression, but who can say?

When I was growing up, my father owned a home heating oil business, which he sold the year I left for college. When I was in grade school, he would sometimes take me with him on service calls. In order to keep me occupied, he'd hand me a screwdriver and tell me to tighten any loose screws I could find on the outside of the furnace—a charge I took on with a deep sense of mission. When my father was deeply concentrated on a difficult physical task, his face would freeze in a grin so like a smile that one time, holding the flashlight for him as he tried to remove some malfunctioning part of an oil burner, I started to chuckle as if we were sharing a joke. He wiped his brow. "What?" he said.

From the time I left for college, all through my twenties and thirties, I longed to know him better. When I could get him alone, I would ask him questions about his life, his troubled relationship with his own father, the early years with my mother, the times during my childhood when it looked like they might separate. Though there was more than a little aggression in my questions, as if I wanted to crack him open and see what was inside, he never seemed offended by my cross-examinations, just a little bewildered. He told me he couldn't remember any of the emotionally difficult times in his life, only the happy ones.

When my grandmother died, my father, who had just had an operation on his ankle, could not travel to attend her funeral. Instead, he wrote a eulogy and sent it to his sister to read aloud at the service in his absence. That night, when I spoke to him on the phone, he told me he wished he could have been there to read it himself. Thinking it would do him some good, I asked him to read it aloud to me.

It was a beautiful eulogy, simple, brief, and moving. He had a difficult time getting through it and broke down several times, each time apologizing for weeping over the death of his own mother. And I, who had spent a good part of my adult life trying to be more emotionally available and expressive, thought of his tears as a good thing, a release.

Not long afterward, I told Lisa's stepfather, David, about the phone call. Like my father, David was a businessman, bluff, genial, and hard to read. When he heard that my father had cried, David grunted, shook his head, and said it was a damned shame. That brought me up short. I'm sure David only meant to say that he was sorry for my father's loss, but suddenly I wondered whether my father's tears, which seemed to me a victory—not just a breakdown but a breakthrough—were, to my father, a defeat.

Over many years of trial and error, when my father lapsed into silence, my mother came to realize that the very worst thing she could do was to try to cheer him up. Instead, she learned, it was best to let him be—or, if she did approach him, to do so obliquely rather than head-on. Lisa and I finish our sandwiches in silence; then she tells me she's going to go back and spend a little more time in the Cathedral. Would I like to come along? I manage an affirmative grunt.

Guidebooks refer to León Cathedral as "The House of Light," second only to Chartres for its stained glass—about 1,800 square meters of it, almost half an acre. In the cool stillness, we stroll beneath the traceries of soaring stone and the impossibly delicate rose windows. Try as I might, it is difficult to wallow when everything around me is shooting, straining, aching skyward. Lisa touches my hand and points out a line of scallop shells in the stonework. "Look," she says. "That's us!"

By and by, I come out of my stupor and reestablish contact with the outside world. For future reference, I provide Lisa with a demonstration of how to read my moods, a field guide, as it were, to my various facial expressions. "Now pay close attention," I say. "Here's me, *furious*." I assume the attitude of Easter Island statuary. "And this is what I look like when I'm *overjoyed*." Same statuary. "Not to be confused with my *wistful* face," (same statuary) "as I pine for the days of my youth . . ."

We find a shoe store near the parador, a tiny space crammed floor to ceiling with boxes. They make a great ceremony of measuring Lisa's much-abused feet and produce, with a flourish, a pair of pink and white running shoes, made in Vietnam. Standing in the middle of the shoe store, in her new shoes, Lisa blinks back tears; it is the first time in weeks that she is able to stand up without pain.

The bouts of emotional paralysis notwithstanding, I do feel refreshed by our furlough in León. And, as we enter the home stretch of the Camino, Lisa's a new peregrina. It's not just that she loves her zippy new shoes; the parador has instilled in her a new vision of what travel could be. Though we may not find another place to match the Hotel San Marcos, she sees somewhere in our future the hazy outline of another *hotel paraíso*. As we set out from León—only two more days' walk to Astorga, at the base of the Montes de León, and we will have left the plains behind us—Lisa has a new mantra: parador, *paradoooor . . .*

5.

fter Astorga, the terrain is suddenly mountainous, a bone-dry, rocky landscape reminiscent of Greece. The trail twists, climbs, and plunges. Goats forage on the steep slopes. Lisa's in pain again. Going uphill isn't a problem, but every downhill step makes her wince. The blisters aren't nearly as bad, but, as if by a law of physics—the Conservation of Torture—now she's got shin splints. "When we get home," she says as she stumps along, "I'm going to get in the *car* and I'm going to *drive* to see a movie in a movie theater. In fact, I'm going to the *Cineplex Odeon* and I'm going to buy a tub of buttered *popcorn* and a Diet Coke with ice which I will order for *myself* in *English* thankyouVERYmuch. And then I'm going to drive home. And then, the next day, I'm going to do it again. Cineplex Odeon. *Ciiinepleeeex Oooodeooon.*"

The path we are walking now is older than Christianity. As long as humans have inhabited the Iberian Peninsula, the way across these mountains has not changed, and there is evidence that—from here on—this pilgrimage is, underneath, as pagan as it is Christian. The original destination on this route was not the insignificant village of Compostela but a more spectacular terminus another two days' walk further on: Finisterre, the westernmost point of Europe, literally the end of the world, where the sun sinks into the ocean. Beyond, there be dragons.

Near Foncebadón, an abandoned village in a mountain pass about a hundred miles east of Santiago, the Camino reaches its highest altitude. In order to ensure safe passage through the realm of the mountain gods, it was customary among the Celtiberians, who came to this part of the world as early as 2,600 years ago, to deposit stones at these high places. There is still an enormous pile of stones at the apex of this mountain pass, and many pilgrims on the Way of Saint James also carry stones—some bring them all the way from home—to add to the mound. Like so many other pagan rituals, the Church has absorbed this one, painted it over with just the thinnest veneer of Christian connotation. The great mound of stones is now topped with an iron cross on a flimsy wooden pole, like a conquistador's flag planted on the beach of a world unimaginably old and strange. No mention of appeasing the mountain gods now; according to the guidebooks, the stones we pilgrims lay on the mound represent our sins, or perhaps our burdens.

We have no stones from home, but we do have Claire's beads. Lisa lays them at the top of the mound of stones, at the base of the cross, and we sit silent for a while, thinking of Cori and Blake, who fell from the sky. And Claire.

We don't stay long. This is a raw, windswept place, more sky than earth, a place to pass through, not to linger. It does not occur to us to ask why the village has been abandoned. Who could live here?

■   ■   ■

Five days to Santiago. Descending into the province of Galicia is like diving into a lake on a scorching summer day. One moment, you're teetering on the high bare rocks, and the next you're below the tree line and in another element altogether. The parched eye drinks in the dappled green country lanes, lined with ancient chestnut trees, small farmyards on either side. Once again, the chorus of chained half-feral dogs, whining, cringing, yelping. The contrapuntal staccato of chickens. The air fecund with cooking smells, mown hay, compost, manure, and blood—at one of the first farms we come to, we witness a hog being slaughtered.

From here on, the food becomes more varied: fresh vegetables, good bread, and now, in all the bars, octopus. Though the idea of eating something with tentacles has never particularly appealed to me, I've always adhered to my father's rule: try the local specialty. Following his swaggering man-of-the-world lead, I've eaten more than my fair share of disgusting objects. Roast pigeon is certainly at the top of the list: served with great ceremony at an expensive English restaurant, it proved to have very little meat on the bones, and what there was of it was grayish-brown and tasted pretty much like you'd expect a rat with wings to taste. My father didn't get far with his portion either; we looked at each other and then, poker-faced co-conspirators that we were, turned simultaneously to my mother and each offered her a tiny forkful: "Here, you've got to try this."

I've tried octopus before, at a formal dinner with other professors from a Japanese university. My first and only bite put up such a valiant resistance to my attempts to chew it that, rather than losing face by spitting it out, I considered swallowing it whole. It tasted like a filthy piece of blown-out truck tire. I've no reason to think that the octopus over here will be any different; even the Spanish name is unpromising: *pulpo*.

However, I've been told that the octopus in Galicia is a delicacy, and as my father's son, I feel honor-bound to try it. Psyching myself up, I tell Lisa I can't wait to get me some cephalopod. It's a schoolyard boast, like telling her I've got worm jelly on my sandwich, and her face screws up satisfyingly in girly disgust.

Of course, when we sit down to dinner, now that I've committed, I have to follow through. The waitress brings me a wooden bowl brimming with steaming chunks of purple-and-white flesh, each piece of tentacle speckled on one side with small white suckers. The thinnest segment, the very end of a tentacle, rises from the center of the bowl beckoning like an extraterrestrial finger. Lisa crosses her arms, leans back in her chair, and waits. I take a long cold swallow of white wine and pick up my fork.

Fortunately for me, it's delicious, drizzled with olive oil, dusted with paprika, delicate in both flavor and texture, like fresh small scallops. Over the next three days, I order *pulpo* several times, and each time I do, I get to smack my lips and rave about it to Lisa. Harpooning yet another chunk on my fork, I hold it out to her: "C'mon, just a no-thank-you bite . . ."

■　　■　　■

As the distance to Santiago shortens, so do my journal entries. Just the facts now: the meals, the miles, the towns, and the fights. What do we fight about? What do all married people fight about? Trivia, mostly. And under the trivia, there are the usual Big Issues: money, sex, responsibility. And under the Big Issues are the Real Issues, things that go back to childhood, or perhaps, depending on your cosmology, the life before this one. So here we are in the home stretch, covering the miles, trying to burn off a little more karma before we reach the end of the world. We quarrel in O Cebreiro. We bicker in Portomarín. We snap at each other in Palas de Rey.

It's not that we aren't enjoying one another's company; our fights, ever shorter, are squalls in an otherwise temperate climate. Still, it's plain that we're both a little irritable. I ask Lisa why she thinks this is, and she replies without hesitation: it's the walking—enough with the walking already.

But for me, it's not the walking. I'm used to it now, the pedestrian life: bandaged feet, sunburn, shouting bikers, cigarette smoke, weird food, cheap hotel rooms, and all, I like it out here. It's not the path that bothers me but the prospect of its end. For a solid month now, I've been unidirectional: a pilgrim, a man with a destination. Upon reaching that destination, however, it seems to me I will have walked myself right out of a job. What will I be then? An unemployed pilgrim.

I tell Lisa that I might just keep walking beyond Santiago, following the ancient route all the way to the sea. I ask her if she'd consider continuing on to Finisterre with me. She nods: "Finisterre? Sure. You go ahead and walk to Finisterre, and I'll meet you there. Know why? Because I'm going to *drive*. In fact, from now on, any time I want to go *anywhere*, I'm going to get in a car, and I am going to *drive* there."

We walk by a café where a cluster of French bikers are loudly toasting each other with glasses of red wine. With luck, they'll be in Santiago before nightfall. (Without luck, at the rate they're drinking, they'll be roadkill.) They're dressed in tiny Speedos, wraparound sunglasses, and not much else. "Boys and their equipment," Lisa mutters.

■　　■　　■

In Arzua, we check into the Hotel Suiza, a pleasant enough place with absolutely nothing Swiss about it. The taciturn man at the front desk stamps our *credenciales* with the seal of his hotel and gravely hands them back to us. It would be a solemn moment except that, behind him, there is a large cage, and in that large cage is a large parrot. "¡Hola!" it shrieks, and bobs its head in energetic sideways figure eights. "¡Hola!"

Santiago is only twenty-three miles away. After all we've been through,

Lisa and I can barely believe we're so close. We could split the distance into a couple of easy anticlimactic days, but we've decided to do the rest of the Camino tomorrow in one last big slog. We're a little giddy. It's going to be hard to get to sleep tonight. For our evening's pilgrim entertainment, we take turns imitating the parrot: bob, bob, "¡Hola! ¡Hola!—braaaack!"

By four in the morning we're on the road. It's full dark, a clear night but moonless. We've managed to slip past the enthusiastic Spanish parrot, but for all our stealth, we still can't leave town without setting off every dog alarm in a half-mile radius. Worried that we'll lose our way on the unlit pilgrim's footpath, we've decided to walk to the next town by following the highway instead. This proves more difficult than we had anticipated; the shoulder of the road is narrow, and it takes a while for our eyes to become sufficiently adjusted to the dark that we can actually see where we're putting our feet. When passing trucks catch us in their high-beams, we stand frozen like deer, and then we have to pause for a few moments to regain both our night vision and our nerve. At Salceda, three miles later, in the deep blue of early dawn, we gratefully step off the highway and back onto the path.

We have breakfast at a bar with maritime decor: fishing floats and nets hanging from the ceiling, a ship's bell behind the bar. We're the only ones in the place besides the barman. He's got Santana on the CD player—"Oye Como Va"—and he's cheerfully singing along as he wipes down the tables. I've always wanted to figure out the lyrics to the song, so I listen closely, but the barman's rendition of the song, like mine, is: "Oye Como Va . . . hmm hmm hmm . . . da da da da DA." When I tip him on the way out, he rings the ship's bell.

Fed and caffeinated, we enjoy the rest of the morning's walk, farm country alternating with fragrant eucalyptus groves. By noon, however, the farms have given way to suburbs and we're about ready to be done for the day. That's when we come to a road sign that says Santiago, seemingly indicating that we've reached the city limits. But the sign, the first of many similar signs we will see today, is a cruel hoax; it's still many miles to the Cathedral. I know this because, by now, I've got a pretty good sense of how long, on average, it takes us to walk a given distance. Considering our timorous predawn starting pace, and figuring in meals and rests, there's no way we're getting to the real Santiago before two or three in the afternoon. However, the road sign has overstimulated the whiny child in the back seat of my mind, and now he will be neither quieted nor distracted. I scrutinize every feature of the landscape, hoping for some indication that we are about to arrive. And so, every bend in the path, every rise, every vista, is a fresh disappointment.

The last hill before Santiago is called the Monte do Gozo—Mount Joy. It is traditional for the members of each band of pilgrims to compete with one another for the honor of being the first to see the spires of Santiago Cathedral. The winner could demand that others in his group refer to him as "the King." (I've found no historical mention of a woman ever winning the contest or claiming this privilege.) His companions might present him with a gift, a coronet of flowers, for example—and later that night, in retribution, they might also present his Highness with the bar tab from the arrival celebration. Some winners took the honor seriously enough—or perhaps just liked the experience so well—that they took King as a nickname, or even a surname, from that day forward. Some say this practice accounts for the prevalence of the name, in various languages, throughout Europe: Rex, Koenig, Kaiser, Leroy, etc.

I imagine that, among the more aggressive of the able-bodied peregrinos, the last day's walk could become a series of short and desperate footraces. Each time the group would come to a hill, no one in the group would know whether *this* hill would turn out to be *the* hill, the Monte do Gozo, and so the fleet of foot, as if vying with one another for their place in heaven, would fling their cloaks aside and sprint to the top, poking at one another with their staffs. Boys and their equipment.

Lisa and I are not about to run any footraces. Just as I think we must surely be getting close to the final hill, the path starts to turn back on itself in odd switchbacks like none we've seen before on the route. I've lost my sense of direction. Within the past fifteen minutes, it seems to me, the sun has been in front of me, behind me, to my left, and to my right. How is this possible? *You're walking in* CIRCLES, shouts my inner brat. *We'll* NEVER *get there.*

Of course, eventually, we do reach the top of Joy Mountain. The afternoon has turned hot and muggy, and it's hard to make out where the city is in the haze, let alone the Cathedral spires. Still disoriented, I approach some other grumpy-looking pilgrims. "Santiago?" I ask, and make the universal palms-up sign for "What the hell?" They grunt and gesture vaguely in a westerly direction. No joy here, but there is a vendor with Cokes on ice. We sit in the shade and cool off for a while before our descent into Santiago.

The city has expanded far beyond its original boundaries, its edge marked not by its medieval walls but by its modern four-lane ring road. To reach the old city, the contemporary peregrino has to make his way by a cement sidewalk alongside the truck route. It's a brutal walk: glaring sun, cinderblock, and diesel fumes. On a highway overpass, yet another sign proclaims that we have reached Santiago. Our first impression of the town is that it is a uniform gray, streets crammed with industrial buildings, offices, and garages.

At last, the gate to the old city. We step through it, and we're in a completely different world, no asphalt, no cars, no engine roar. Slate paving stones, narrow, gently curving streets with porticoes, wrought iron balconies, small shops, ornately carved wooden doors, ocher stone walls.

In our pilgrim band of two, I have the honor of being the first to see the Cathedral spires. "You may call me Leroy," I say to Lisa. She does not respond.

6.

The Camino approaches the Catedral de Santiago from the east, and so the first entrance we come to is not the grand western facade but a smaller portal on the north side. We step inside, but arriving by the side entrance feels all wrong to me, and before my eyes can adjust to the dim interior, I do an about-face. We've walked four hundred miles to get here, and, pilgrim, we're going to walk in the *front* door, the Pórtico de Gloria.

So, in the first of several "do-overs" we will perform in the course of our arrival, Lisa and I go back outside and walk around the Cathedral to the center of the vast Plaza del Obradoiro. From there we can take in the whole front of the building, the twin stairs, the three ornate towers, and in the top gable of the central tower, presiding calmly over the riot of baroque stonework below him, the figure of James with his broad-brimmed hat, gourd, and pilgrim's staff.

Over the centuries, each Spanish king has striven to outdo his predecessors with improvements to this building, the final resting place of the country's patron saint. The original modest Romanesque church, built to house the reliquary, has long disappeared, and the gothic structure that swallowed it has, in turn, nearly been swallowed by various baroque additions and renovations. Inside and out, the Cathedral of Saint James is a thrice-gilded lily.

I've been here once before, on a trip with my mother and father. Fifteen, hormonal, and impossibly opinionated, I hated this cathedral. Compared with other cathedrals I'd seen in England and France, I found this one ridiculous, gaudy, and utterly incoherent. But it is one thing to arrive in Santiago as a sullen teenager stuffed into the back of your parents' rental car, quite another to reach this destination as a bona fide footsore pilgrim. Yes, as architecture, the Cathedral is excessive. At fifteen, easily embarrassed by any excess, especially those of my parents, I couldn't stand it. But at thirty-eight, it seems just about right; anything less demonstrative would be disappointing.

Lisa turns to me. "You ready?" I am.

We cross the square, climb the stairs, pass through the Portal of Glory, and we are engulfed by the Cathedral. Many things in life are disappointing. This walk, up the long center aisle of the nave, to the sanctuary and the high altar, is not one of them.

I am still a stranger in a strange land indeed, a Quaker among the Catholics, but both Lisa and I have the sense that, at least for this moment, we've earned the right to be here. A cathedral is an odd place to be proud of yourself; everything about this canyon of stone, this vast pile of devotional ornament, is meant to be humbling, a reminder that we are here only by the grace of God. But in the Cineplex Odeon of my mind, as we limp toward the altar, this is the scene in the Western where the badass heroes (with their scallop-shell badges) swagger into the saloon as if they own the place. And all you can hear is the chink of our spurs.

The place is full of Japanese and German tourists. Somehow, we did not expect this. What are tourists doing here? They look phony and out of place. Now us, we *belong* here. We've got the packs, the scallop shells, the staffs, the scabby feet, the thousand-yard stare, the pilgrim reek. We're the real deal. Step aside, amigos: peregrinos coming through.

■　　■　　■

It takes more than a day to properly *arrive* in Santiago. There is much to do. To begin with, there's the bewildering series of rituals pilgrims are expected to perform. We've read about some of them in advance, but it seems to us that, wherever we go in the Cathedral, we are directed—either by the guidebook we've picked up from the gift shop or by other pilgrims—to yet another small ceremony.

Start at the altar: it contains two sets of stairs. One set leads up behind the gilded statue of Saint James, and you are expected to embrace him and thank him for bringing you safely to Santiago. I give it a try, but the sensation of hugging this big hunk of metal is so odd that I can't bring myself to do it with any feeling. A quick clinch, as if I'm about to begin a wrestling match with a robot; I straighten up and pause for a moment. Okay, that's done—I'm down the stairs on the other side before I realize that I've forgotten to pray. Do-over. Second try, I take my time, which doesn't reduce the strangeness, but when I step down, at least I feel I might have gotten off a decent thank-you to the James-O-Matic.

The other set of stairs leads down to the crypt where, through a small window, you can view the silver and gold casket containing the remains of Saint James. I read in the guidebook that there is some physical evidence supporting, if not the miraculous rediscovery of the bones, at least the antiquity of this site as a burial ground. Archeologists, excavating the space below the present-day crypt, have discovered another tomb dating from approximately the first century. And though I know the bones in the casket before me are supposed to have the power to work miracles, this particular part of the ritual feels only mildly significant, like viewing a sarcophagus in a museum. It's a fancy box. If there's bones in there, they are some pretty old bones. Yep. Old bones. Old. Bones.

We visit all the side chapels, built in various eras and dedicated to a bewildering array of saints, patrons, and manifestations of the Virgin. (Our Lady of the Snows?) Lisa lights a candle below a particularly sympathetic and maternal figure of Mary. For good measure, trying once again to make peace with the image, I light a candle below a remarkably gory depiction of James the Moor-Slayer on horseback trampling and hacking down the hordes of the enemy with his terrible swift sword. Glory Halleluiah.

Next. A stone statue of a curly-haired young man genuflects in prayer facing the altar—as if he has just stumbled through the doors and fallen to his knees in gratitude. Pilgrims refer to him as the "Santo do Croques," though both the origin and the actual meaning of the name are unclear. Of the two traditional explanations in the guidebook, the more plausible (or so it seems to me) is that the word *croque* derives from the Provençal word for "curl"—and that the statue is the "Curly-Haired Saint." But plausibility and pilgrimage do not often walk hand in hand. In Galician, the local dialect, *croque* refers to "a blow to the head." Taking the latter translation literally, it has become customary for the arriving pilgrim to kneel before the statue and knock heads with it.

I'm game, so I step up to the statue. But when I actually kneel to butt heads with Saint Curly, I do have a faint suspicion that I've been had. Maybe the next thing I'll be directed to do as part of this pilgrim hazing will be to get poked in the eyes by Saint Larry or Saint Moe. *That's it*, I think, *I'm done for the day.*

But then, on our way out, Lisa and I pause for one last ritual. We stand before a column depicting the family tree of King David, its branches twisting, climbing, and flowering, generation upon generation until, at the top, strange fruit, the figures of Mary and Jesus spring from the Old Testament foliage. Our guidebook tells us that it is customary for pilgrims to put their fingers between the branches, and that, by so doing, we will "receive as many mercies as there are fingers on both hands."

Near the base of the column, clearly recognizable: a handprint. A handprint not carved, but *worn* deep into the elaborate stone fretwork by the hands of nameless millions of pilgrims over hundreds of years. As I fit my right hand into this print, and in taking it away I wear away some infinitesimal share of the stone, it seems to me, for the first time, that Lisa and I are participating, not just in the form of a pilgrim ritual, but in a true sacrament, a communion, palm-to-palm, with all the pilgrims who have come before us and all the pilgrims who have yet to arrive.

7.

The next day, our first task is to secure our Compostela from the Pilgrim Office. We've got our credencial stamped and ready and, just in case, my letter from the Abbot, but we're a little nervous. What if they question us about our religious faith? What if they've found out about the taxi ride into Burgos? What if, after coming all this way, they tell us we have to bring them the broomstick from the Wicked Witch of the West? We find the building near the Cathedral and, steeling ourselves for a Spanish inquisition, climb the stone staircase to the second-floor office. The young monk behind the counter bids us good morning, and, in Spanish, I introduce myself and Lisa as peregrinos from the United States inquiring, if he pleases, whether he might be so good as to grant us a Compostela. He listens gravely as one might to a six-year-old and then, to my great relief, responds in fluent English. Examining our credencial, he asks why we've made the journey: was it for religious purposes or cultural? I stammer out that our intent was, in part, spiritual. He pauses for a moment and gazes at me with mock severity.

Then he says, "Okay," and whips out a couple of Compostelas from under the counter. I tell him I'd like one document made out in both our names, and he turns to Lisa with a raised eyebrow and asks, "And what do you want?" Lisa, who for the last month has been unable to communicate her needs and opinions to anyone but me, says, "That's what I want too." He asks if we're married, and Lisa pipes up, "We're *very* married." At this, he smiles, writes our names into the Compostela, and turns it around for us to inspect. It says:

CAPITULUM hujus Almae Apostolicae et Metropolitanae Ecclesiae Compostellanae sigilli Altaris Beati Jacobi Apostoli custos, ut omnibus Fidelibus et Perigrinis ex toto terrarum Orbe, devotionis affectu vel voti causa, ad limina Apostoli Nostri Hispaniarum Patroni ac Tutelaris SANCTI JACOBI convenientibus, authenticas visitationis litteras expediat, omnibus et singulis praesentes inspecturis, notum facit: <u>Davidem Hlavsa et Elisabetham Holtby</u>. Hoc sacratissimum Templum pietatis causa devote visitasse. In quorum fidem praesentes litteras, sigillo ejusdem Sanctae Ecclesiae munitas, ei confero. Datum Compostellae die <u>16</u> mensis <u>Iunius anno Dei 2000</u>. Canonicus Deputatus pro Peregrinis

Lisa takes one look at our new Compostela and blurts out, "But that's not my name!" I put my hand on her arm. "Honey, it's in Latin. That's your name in Latin." "Oh," she says to the monk, blushing, "sorry."

Having obtained our honorable discharge from the pilgrim corps, we spend the morning decommissioning ourselves. Leaving packs, scallop shells, and other pilgrim paraphernalia behind, we stroll the narrow streets and arcades off the plaza, where we procure civilian clothing and sandals. (In one shop, much waving of hands as I try to explain to the salesladies what kind of undergarments Lisa requires. Hilarity ensues.) We exit each store wearing our purchases; by late morning, all of our pilgrimwear has been stowed in shopping bags, and we are, head to toe, down to the skin, in mufti. To complete the renovation, I visit a barber who clips my hair down to its usual quarter-inch buzz cut and flirts with Lisa as he shaves my neck with a straight razor.

■   ■   ■

We've lost track of time—it is nearly noon, time for the daily Pilgrim Mass. No time to drop off our shopping bags: we head straight for the Cathedral, across the open plaza under the blazing sun, and coming through the doors just as the processional music begins, we stand at the back for a moment blinking, orienting ourselves. The center section of the nave is nearly full, and we can see that most of the attendees sitting in the pews are not pilgrims but regular congregants, mostly elderly women in black. We try to slip unobtrusively into a back pew, but just as we are about to sit down, an attendant takes me by the elbow, asking what country we're from and at what point on the Camino we began our pilgrimage. I stammer out a reply, and he jots down the information, hustles us up to the front row, and motions for the other pilgrims to make space for us and our shopping bags. So much for inconspicuousness. We are two blushing pilgrims. All the others in our pew look like they've been out overcoming enemy hordes with their staffs, getting properly chastised and reformed by their packs and whatnot. Us, we've been shopping.

Lisa turns to me and whispers: "How did he know we were peregrinos?" I shrug; I don't know either. But then it occurs to me that, looking at us, it wouldn't take a supersleuth to guess that we're fresh off the trail. Maybe our bandaged feet gave us away, or our south-facing sunburns. Or maybe it's that our apparel still bears the odd geometrical creases of clothing just off the shelf.

The priest climbs into the pulpit and, as part of the greeting of the faithful, reads the list compiled by the attendants: most of the pilgrims sitting with us are from Spain and France, but there are also a scattering of Brazilians, Germans, and Italians. Lisa and I are the only Americans. Everyone has walked at least sixty miles; a few have walked ten times that.

Some believe the name Compostela derives from a joining of the Latin words for field (*campus*) and star (*stella*), but I find it more plausible that the town was named for its Roman burial ground and that it derives not from a joining of earth and sky but from compost, which is, after all, what you smell like when you arrive. The last town you pass through before you reach Santiago is named Lavacolla, which may be loosely translated as "wash your tail"—a special consideration before entering the holy city. On arrival, the priests are glad to bless the pilgrims, sure, but the true purpose of the Pilgrim Mass is fumigation.

And fumigation, it turns out, is the main reason we pilgrims are directed to the front pews. Unlike the regular parishioners in the rows further back—who are aware of what is about to happen to us—we are seated at the intersection of nave and transept, the very center of the cruciform Cathedral, directly under the great dome. I tilt my head back and look straight up at the apex of the dome, and a triangular painting of the unblinking eye of God—much like the creepy, disembodied eye on the back of the dollar bill—stares down at me. From God's perspective, the peregrino must appear much like the cartoon character who, instructed to stand on the big X, gamely obeys. Overhead, between us and the eyeball, a slender ironwork bridge stretches from one side of the dome to the other. Suspended from the center of the bridge, a rope dangles from a pulley, not straight down but, for now, pulled to the side and secured at the base of a column. *What's that for?* I wonder.

The Catedral de Santiago is home to the Botafumeiro, which, five feet tall and weighing in at 176 pounds, is one of the world's largest incense burners. Midway through the service, as a nun steps up to a wooden lectern and begins to sing a lovely plainsong, eight men in red robes, the *tiraboleiros*, carry in the giant solid silver censer, attach it to the rope, and fill its central chamber with hot coals and incense. Fragrant smoke pours from the sides of the Botafumeiro, and, with a gentle push, one of the tiraboleiros sets it swinging from side to side. Without interrupting her song, the nun takes a step backward and pulls her lectern with her.

By rhythmically tugging on the rope, the octet of tiraboleiros gradually increase the sweep of the pendulum until the Botafumeiro, swinging from one side of the transept to the other, becomes a flaming, smoking comet—reaching a maximum arc two hundred feet across and seventy feet high. From where I sit, it seems as if each pass of the censer comes within inches of knocking the singing nun from her lectern like a golf ball from a tee. She doesn't miss a note.

I try to reassure myself that the men in red are trained professionals, but it's hard to believe these crazy Spaniards don't take out a peregrino or two now and then. (*Bam! ¡Hasta luego!*) And friends, let me tell you, we aren't the only pilgrims who cringe each time the sizzling Botafumeiro whooshes past. By the third or fourth pass, the Frenchman sitting next to us has nearly crawled into Lisa's lap.

Once they've decelerated, snuffed, and stowed the Flaming Pendulum of Death, I can't help but think the rest of the service is going to be a bit of an anticlimax, and I don't envy the priest. But his sermon—which is about seeking God in the ordinary, about life as a pilgrimage, and about taking the passion of James as a believer into our daily lives—sticks with me. Your real pilgrimage, says the priest, doesn't end here in Santiago; your real pilgrimage *starts* here.

At least I think that's the general drift of what he is saying—he is, after all, speaking Spanish-that-has-nothing-to-do-with-food, and I'm still in an adrenaline state from our fumigation.

When it's over, we stand at the top of the steps, stunned, looking out over the plaza. Lisa asks me if I'm really still planning to walk on to Finisterre. I shake my head. "No, I'm done walking," I tell her; "we've arrived." After a while, when it doesn't look like I'm going to move, Lisa takes my arm. "Come on," she says gently, and we stroll around the old city with no particular place to go.

. ■ .

One more thing left to do: we rent a car the next day, an underpowered boxy model of uncertain provenance that both looks and drives like a giant gold-plated toaster on wheels. Finisterre is three days' hard walk from Santiago, but at seventy miles per hour (with the other cars on the superhighway blazing past us) it's a short, if harrowing, drive. High on the rocky point stands a whitewashed lighthouse with a small café, a gift shop, and a foghorn so powerful that it must rival Gabriel's trumpet. The blasts of this horn, which don't seem to faze the proprietor, are spaced just far enough apart so that visitors cannot anticipate exactly when the next one is coming. As such, with each new apocalypse of sound, we pilgrims jerk and squawk like startled chickens.

Lisa and I clamber around the rocks between the lighthouse and the sheer drop to the ocean. We find the remains of several campfires, some of which include the charred remnants of sandals, boots, and clothing. I imagine the evidence of these small conflagrations might seem mysterious to nonperegrinos, even ominous—as if visitors to this promontory were particularly susceptible to spontaneous combustion—but we know what's happened. Perhaps we too should stage a ritual burning of our fetid pilgrim clothing. With all the rituals we've been through since we came to Santiago, I still don't feel I've quite made the transition to civilian life. We've already been smoked, but maybe a burning would help.

A haze blurs the line between water and sky, obliterating the horizon. I position our camera on a rock ledge, press the timer button, and take a picture of us—Lisa and me suspended, in the days when we were still childless, floating in the blue-gray void at the end of the world.

We pause at the gift shop on the way out. Lisa and I have been looking for souvenirs to bring home as gifts for our family and friends, but here, as in the other souvenir shops and stands we've browsed, there's plenty to buy and nothing we want. All along the Camino Francés, you can buy souvenirs: Santiago dessert spoons, iron-on scallop shell patches, bracelets of yellow-arrow beads, tea towels with the cross of Saint James, bottles of "peregrino ointment," "Ultreya" T-shirts. This is not to mention the various dishes, mugs, caps, purses, soaps, lapel pins, pendants, crosses, figurines, rosaries, key rings, statuettes, and—very Spanish, this—Camino de Santiago cigarette lighters.

I think I understand why people buy these things. I suppose that every newly arrived pilgrim faces the same difficulty we're facing: the sudden and overwhelming conviction that something needs to be shared with people back home, something important, and it's going to be hard to explain. Words will fail, so you want to have something to hand people, some tangible piece of the experience. But we haven't found anything suitable, and I'm thinking we may just have to come back empty-handed.

South of the rocky point, there is a broad, sandy beach and a weathered, low cinderblock restaurant with a terrace where they serve cold white wine and grilled fish just pulled from the sea. Spanish families sit at the other tables; a grandmother leans back in her chair as mother and father put in their orders for food and shoo their bouncing children away from the table until it's time to eat. The morning mist has dissipated; the sky is clear, the air mild, the water so placid that we can barely hear the lap of the waves. The kids play soccer with a beach ball. The rest of us sit becalmed in the early afternoon sun, staring at the horizon, sipping wine, and waiting for our fish.

And then the beach ball hits grandma upside the head. I don't know why, but this seems to me very Spanish.

When we're done eating, Lisa and I take off our sandals, walk across the beach, and wade into the warm water up to our knees. And there we find the solution to our souvenir problem. At our feet, tiny scallop shells, delicate, pink, white, gray, tan, hundreds of them—treasure scattered across the sands. And so, just as pilgrims have done for the last millennium, we scoop up as many as we can hold to take home to the people we love.

Three more days until our flight home. When you've come to the end of the world, what do you do then?

I don't know, but Lisa has an idea: paradors.

When what you're seeking is luxury, it's easy to be disappointed in small things. We hop in the golden toaster and drive to Baiona where we stay in a majestic four-star parador in a seaside castle. The three-star parador in Pontevedra, by contrast, is less than satisfying: another castle, yes, but this one's in town, you see, and it just won't do. One of our dinners is overlong and accompanied by an endlessly looping Elvis CD, which is charming the first time through, but palls upon repetition. Lisa's chilly in the evenings, and no matter how hard we shop, we can't find her a proper sweater. No, it's five stars or nothing, so we return to Santiago and check into El Hostal de Los Reyes Católicos, the oldest hotel in the world. This passes muster.

Sipping brandy, I sit with Lisa in the café on the plaza, gazing up at the moon between the Cathedral spires. Not bad. Still I am uneasy; I can feel the old soporific fog creeping back in. Having come all this way in a straight line, I can't shake off the suspicion that I've gone full circle. We're not pilgrims anymore; we're tourists.

I hate being a tourist.

8.

As soon as our plane touched down on American soil, Lisa perked right up. As we waited in the Philadelphia airport for our connection to Seattle, and, for the first time in many weeks, were surrounded by people who spoke English, my wife, now no longer helpless and with an excellent command of the native language, strode around the airport striking up conversations, smiling, nodding, listening intently to what people had to say, loaning them pens and pencils, giving directions, and even carrying their bags for them. I hope she didn't frighten anyone, my Friendliest Girl on speed. She was just so glad to be *useful* again.

A friend picked us up at Sea-Tac. A short sprint up the interstate, and in no time, we found ourselves on the curb in front of our building. Lisa produced the house key she had stored in one of her pack's secret inner pockets. One moment, we were in loud, smoky, vibrant, bloody Spain, and then the next, there we were, back in our living room. I put down my pack and perched on the edge of the couch. As Lisa bustled around our calm, quiet, gray apartment, unpacking, raising the shades, opening the windows, I stared at our furniture, our floor, our *stuff*. *Where* am *I?* I wondered.

Before we left for Spain, I had committed to overseeing a summer theater program at the University. Normally, on returning from vacation, I would tuck into such a task with gusto, but now the job was simply an irritant, a constant stream of administrivia. I could scarcely believe that it was my job. As I had feared, it seemed to me I'd been laid off from my real job the moment we arrived in Santiago. When I had to go to the office, I missed Lisa terribly, not with the sweet romantic ache of an absent lover, but with the grief and panic of a man who has lost his bearings. I would call her once or twice during the day, not to say anything in particular, but just to sit for a moment and reorient myself. Eager for relief, I would return home in the evening, only to find that our apartment no longer felt like home.

At night or in the morning, in the twilight and dawning of my waking mind, I would replay the whole of the Camino from the Pyrenees to Santiago. It seemed to me that I could recall and see in my mind's eye every step of the Camino, every turn in the path, every new vista. This conviction stayed with me for months after our return until, inevitably, I could no longer sustain it, and, day by day, I could feel parts of the route decaying and falling away from me.

From time to time, I would try to pray, still not a familiar or comfortable activity for me, and the sermon from the Pilgrim Mass in Santiago Cathedral would come to mind. I would try to apply what the priest had said about seeking the divine in my ordinary life, but I was having a terrible time: I could find no passion worthy of the name; if life is a pilgrimage, I thought to myself, then I'm sitting it out, squirming in my comfortable chair, here in my one-bedroom parador. And there's not even a minibar.

I wanted to get back on the road, so to speak, to embark on the next part of the pilgrimage. Destination: house and baby. *Ultreya, already.* But when I brought this up with Lisa, she suggested that I should maybe try to calm down a little. She had no desire to go back to the clinic, not yet, and she wasn't ready to start house hunting—not now, not when it's summer in Seattle. She had a point: if you live in Seattle, you really do need to take advantage of the summer, when the days are sunny, the air is mild, the flowers bloom in giddy profusion, the mountains shine, and the islands beckon. (This in contrast to the Seattle winter, in which every day looks like the inside of a burned-out lightbulb and feels like the underside of a slug.) Once again, time for me to suck it up and for God's sake enjoy myself. So, for the next two weeks, whenever I could avoid going to work, we went for walks, lay about in parks, and, as Lisa had promised herself we would, drove to the Cineplex Odeon to eat popcorn and see perfectly ridiculous summer movies.

■   ■   ■

Then, refreshed, Lisa reengaged her fearsome logistical skills. Halleluiah: forward motion. We put our apartment on the market and, in short order, it sold, leaving us wondering where we were going to live if we didn't find a place by the closing date. We recommenced the French farce of our visits to the fertility clinic, each of us entering and leaving by separate doors and at different times.

A few weeks of suspense, and we found a house we could afford. Built in 1947, it was a solid two-bedroom cottage with a dry basement. It wasn't a "fixer" exactly; theoretically, a spunky youngish couple such as ourselves should be able to renovate and redecorate such a place without being unreasonably dependent on the kindness of contractors. That Lisa and I had no experience with carpentry, plumbing, wiring, masonry, tiling, plastering, gardening, and a host of other skills that are the minimum requirements for embarking on such projects did not deter us.

The elderly couple who owned the house before us had lived there for many years and had clearly given it their time and loving attention. In so doing, they had made many, many unfortunate improvements, some of which—such as covering the original cedar with steel siding—were pretty much irreversible. Other changes were reversible, but would require more time, money, and fortitude than we currently had in stock. For example, the house's original double-hung wood-frame windows had been replaced with hideous double-paned aluminum sliders. Over time, the seals on most of these had failed, allowing moisture to seep in between the double panes. More than one visitor to our house walked up to one of our windows and swept a hand across it only to realize that the fog obscuring the view was *inside* the window. At the bottom of each failed pane, the constant trickle of condensation nurtured a profusion of exotic and colorful molds and fungi.

The property, almost a quarter acre, presented further challenges we were not likely to rise to for some time. Blighted rose bushes, more thorn than flower. An area that had probably once been a garden, now thick with weeds. What must have been the back lawn, now a tawny, blasted patch of heath.

Setting aside the projects we could not yet attempt, Lisa and I set about de-improving as much of the house as we could. First to go: the 1970s vintage orange, brown, and harvest gold shag carpets. De-carpeting revealed that the gorgeous original oak floors, though in need of refinishing, were otherwise in excellent shape. The front stoop had been enclosed, converted to a curious sort of shed/mudroom; I bought my first power tool, a tiger saw, and de-enclosed it. We rented a steamer, and Lisa removed the crumbling mud-brown wallpaper. From the bathroom tub (which would need refinishing), I removed the kitschy swan-patterned glass doors and put up a shower curtain. I spent most of a day removing the various hooks, clips, and other hardware the previous owners had nailed or screwed into every available surface—undoing the effects of decades of "Honey, would you hang this up for me?"

For our tenth wedding anniversary, I had given Lisa a gold ring set with ten tiny diamonds. For our twelfth anniversary, after we had made our separate visits to the clinic for our monthly donation-and-insemination routine, Lisa and I rented a U-Haul and took more than a ton of debris to the dump. At the transfer station, goggled and gloved, Lisa and I lobbed each item from the back of the truck, over the railing, down to the great trash pile twenty feet below: rolls of carpet, dented screen doors, bent metal venetian blinds, dusty curtains, broken boards, splintered sheets of plywood. The shower doors hit the pile with a satisfying splash of glass. You want romantic? That was romantic.

And when we had emptied the place and stripped it down to the walls, when we had scrubbed off as much grime as possible, when at last we had made for ourselves, not yet a home, but a place to make our home, that's when Lisa got pregnant.

9.

isa's elation at finding out that her body was actually capable of conceiving (and with my morphologically challenged sperm, no less) soon gave way to fear—which she kept to herself—that the pregnancy test had been a false positive. But week six brought incontrovertible evidence: Lisa went to the clinic for an ultrasound and returned home with a black-and-white picture.

We put it on the refrigerator: our son, the lima bean.

The chance of miscarriage is high in the first six weeks of pregnancy: according to some estimates, about 25percent; after that, it drops to about 8 percent and then, at twelve weeks, 2 percent. We had resolved to wait until Christmas (week fourteen) to tell our families—Lisa had the idea she would give them little silver-framed copies of an ultrasound baby picture as Christmas gifts—but, with our odds improving and proof positive of Junior's existence on our fridge, we barely made it to Halloween before we began to blurt out the news to close friends. And then it seemed silly to keep it from our parents. My mother and father had been so determined not to be the kind of parents who meddle in their son's marriage that they had never asked whether—let alone when—we might be planning to give them grandchildren already. When I called with the news, they whooped so loud I had to hold the phone away from my ear. Lisa's mother reacted to the news by climbing into Lisa's lap. After phoning Lisa's dad, we swore each other to secrecy until the end of the first trimester.

Human gestation, from conception to birth, takes 266 days, give or take. Home renovation, by contrast, is a process of indeterminate length. The race was on. Counting forward from our wedding anniversary/insemination/dump run, we calculated we'd reach the finish line on or about July 1, 2001. Whatever parts of the nest hadn't been feathered by that point might need to remain featherless for quite some time.

Every wall in the house needed painting, every ceiling, every bit of molding, every shelf, every cabinet, every door and window frame. What didn't need painting needed refinishing, resurfacing, regrouting, recaulking, re-covering, or reupholstering. We needed new appliances, furnishings, fixtures, blinds. This much I could see. But beyond these basics, Lisa's short-term vision for the house included more: laying new marble and granite tile floors in the kitchen and bathroom; replacing the bathroom wainscoting and installing ceramic shower tile, a new toilet, and a pedestal sink; converting our bedroom closet from a murky blind alley into an open space with bifold doors; and changing out the moldy windows in the baby's room.

The baby's room: we were using it as our home office, and that would not do. So, as we had no room for an office upstairs, we'd need to finish the basement. That would mean framing new walls; installing electrical outlets, switches, and overhead lighting; putting in heating ducts; drywalling; building a subfloor; laying linoleum tile; and who knew what else.

And it's not like we weren't already busy. Lisa was teaching her full schedule of yoga classes, now with added commute time back and forth from our old neighborhood, and I was fully engaged in my fall semester—my favorite part of the academic year—which consumed not just my weekdays but parts of my weekends as well. Even considering that I would have a month off around Christmas, a week in spring, and another six weeks after the end of school, I was skeptical that we would be able to accomplish everything on Lisa's list by Junior's arrival date. Far as I was concerned, a home that would keep us and a baby warm and dry would have to do; we'd make improvements as time allowed.

Lisa, quite rightly, resented my being drawn back to work. She had begun to scale back her professional, social, and volunteer commitments as soon as we began house hunting in earnest, and now that she was pregnant, she was doing so even more. I imagine that if she had felt well enough, Lisa might have strapped on the tool belt herself. However, by week four of her pregnancy, Lisa had realized that she would be able to accomplish almost none of the physical work herself and that, once again, as she had all the way across Spain, she would have to depend entirely on me.

■   ■   ■

If pregnancy came with warning label, it might read, in part, "May cause nausea, unremitting fatigue, mental fog, radical mood swings, despair, giddiness, anxiety, irritability, euphoria, humorlessness, abrupt uncontrolled weeping, paranoia, bloating, headaches, flatulence, sciatica, acne, sore breasts, anemia, unexplained food cravings, sleeplessness, hallucinogenic nightmares." Or at least these would have been the warnings on Lisa's label. Your results may vary.

Whenever I was home, as I had in Spain, I fetched and carried for Lisa. When all she could keep down was crackers, I got her a dozen different kinds and built a huge cracker-box pyramid on the kitchen counter. When she needed to talk, I listened. "I'm fat," she would say, and I would tell her how much I loved her pregnant body. "I think I'm a tiny bit depressed," she would say, and I would say, "I think you're a tiny bit pregnant." Evenings, when I wasn't working and the nausea was at bay, we would curl up by the fireplace, and I would read to her or play the guitar. And I would put my head against her belly and talk softly to the baby. Hello, baby.

By week eight, however, when she was at her sickest and witchiest, my attempts to project calm in the face of the impending storm only maddened Lisa further. From her perspective, which she shared with me rather forcefully, everything around her—not excepting her husband—was half-assed and unfinished. Inside, outside, *nothing* was pretty to look at. And there's no good shopping in this hick neighborhood. We might as well be in, in . . . *Nebraska*. The baby needs furniture. And windows you can actually *see* out of. The baby wants *orange juice*. Fresh, from *oranges*, not from a plastic container. And go get me some meat, too. The baby wants *meat*.

Is mama happy? No, she is not. And when mama's not happy, nobody's happy. Time, again, for me to step up. I dropped or deferred several projects I was working on at the University; I cut back on other commitments—Lisa had made it quite clear to me that "quality time" at home would not be enough: sometimes, there's no substitute for quantity. Cracker pyramids and sweet nothings and evenings by the fire were all well and good, but if I really wanted domestic tranquility, I'd best get myself home, strap on the tool belt, pick up the pace, and renovate the hell out of something until it by God didn't need renovating any more.

■ ■ ■

Fortunately, at this point, Lisa's stepfather came to the rescue. A gung ho veteran of numerous home-repair campaigns—with some actual experience working construction—David came over nearly every weekend to lend his time, energy, and expertise. If he didn't know how to do a job himself, it seemed he always had a buddy in the trades he could ask. You don't have to be a pro to do this stuff, he told me, in the first of many pep talks. Most of it is pretty simple, and if your carpentry isn't entirely accurate, if there are gaps in your dry-walling, well, there's always muck!

"Muck?" I asked.

"Caulk, wood filler, putty, wall compound, you know, *muck*. When something's not exactly right, you just *muck it in*."

Despite my misgivings after this conversation, I found that David had a pretty good sense of when a job would be beyond our capabilities as weekend warriors—that is, when amateurism or ignorance might actually cause significant damage or prove dangerous. You don't have to be an expert in hydraulics to install a new faucet, he said, but putting in a new toilet, you probably want a plumber. Wiring the basement? No problem. Upgrading the electrical panel? Problem; get help.

To my relief, I proved reasonably handy at the jobs we took on, but, bless him, David continually talked up my modest attainments to Lisa as if I were a prodigy, a home-repair savant. Able to work eight hours straight with only the occasional short break for a sandwich or a glass of ice water, David had, easily, twice my physical strength and endurance. We kept up a running joke that he and I were contractors, "D&D Construction," working for Lisa. Each time we would make a slight mistake and need to improvise some patch on our work (often, as advertised, with muck), he'd whisper to me, "Just don't tell the owner; she'll never know." Once, when we had completed a job and stood back to admire our work, we decided that we should have business cards made—they'd look just like regular business cards, but when you tried to slip one in your wallet, you'd discover that the corners weren't exactly square.

Week twelve. Lisa had some spotting (aka *bleeding*—oh, not uncommon, chirped the pregnancy books, but *do* have yourself checked out). Terrified, she went straight to the clinic for another ultrasound. The baby was fine, she told me later: a good strong heartbeat, big head, tiny arms waving around. Clever baby! Couldn't tell whether it was a boy or a girl yet, but she felt sure it was a boy. And so, we named him James.

■   ■   ■

The second trimester often brings an easing of the symptoms of morning sickness and a surge of energy. This did not happen for Lisa. But you do what you have to, so Lisa put one foot in front of the other: taught her classes, did her errands and housework, cooked elaborate holiday meals for the relatives, chose the paints, ordered the furniture for the baby's room, coped with the noise, and mopped up the construction dust.

David and I conducted a holiday renovation campaign, a pre-Christmas blitz on the kitchen and a grinding post–New Year's siege on the bathroom, vanquishing the flooring and tiling projects. In the dawn following the last battle, I opened the bathroom door and was nearly blinded by the sun beaming through the pebbled glass of the new window and reflecting off the pristine white tile and porcelain. Lo! Choirs of angels!

Week sixteen. With the rush of the holidays over and D&D Construction on hiatus, Lisa devoted herself to lying quietly, feeling, for the first time, the baby moving, a flutter, a feather touch.

And then, a month later, he was gone.

10.

At twenty weeks, Lisa and I went to the hospital together for a third ultrasound. In the windowless basement imaging room, the technician made small talk and popped his gum as he dimmed the lights. Lisa lay back on the table. I shifted in my seat, jammed my hands in my pockets, and stretched out my legs like a teenager settling in to watch the movie. As the technician slid the paddle around on Lisa's belly, the image on the computer screen wheeled, dipped, and blurred. Finally the baby's image popped into focus, arms and legs folded, resting on his back, as if lying on the bottom of the pool, waiting to spring to the surface.

I said, "Cool."

The technician muttered something, hit a button to freeze the image, and walked briskly out of the room.

A pause. The throb and hiss of subterranean hospital machinery.

Still on the table, Lisa sat up. "What's going on?"

The technician returned, accompanied now by our midwife and a small man wearing a rumpled white coat and steel-rimmed glasses, his bow tie askew. Without introducing himself, the white-coated man shut the door behind him, and as the technician and the midwife stood silently near the door, he came over to us and sat down on a stool. He looked as if someone had left him out in the rain.

I can't remember what the man said, just his imposed calm, the care with which he chose his words. What we had taken for a frozen image, he told us, was in fact mere stillness.

I could tell that he was upset, a little angry, afraid of how we might react–who wants to break such news?—but I found it hard to believe that he was talking about *us*, and so I could neither feel the impact nor register the import of his words. Trying to get my bearings, I looked at Lisa, but I couldn't read her face.

And then the man in the white coat and the technician were gone, and the midwife was explaining that we had a decision to make: Did we want to schedule a D&C or induce labor? Though she spoke plainly enough, I wanted to ask her to slow down. It seemed to me that I had lost my language, that I could not translate fast enough. And then I understood: Did we—she was asking—want the pregnancy to end in the outpatient clinic, a surgical procedure, or in the maternity ward, a stillbirth?

Again, I looked at Lisa, but Lisa said nothing, so I asked whether there were medical advantages or disadvantages to either choice, and the midwife told us, no, it was simply a matter of preference. No hurry. Let us know.

She asked if we had any other questions. I tried to think of one. I wanted to ask a question that would take some thought, some care, some time for the midwife to answer, but I had no such question. Dead is dead.

I said, "Are you sure?"

"Yes," she said, "I'm sorry. We're sure."

■   ■   ■

On the drive home, we were mostly silent. As if exchanging telegrams, Lisa and I said what we needed to and no more. We each assumed there was only one possible decision, so when we talked, we talked logistics: appointments to reschedule, job responsibilities to manage. We thought of the questions we had been too stunned to ask the midwife. How long would Lisa's recovery time be? How long would the procedure itself take? Then we realized we weren't in agreement. I was talking about the D&C, while Lisa had decided to give birth. Incredulous, I asked why she would want to go through all that pain. She said she couldn't imagine just getting rid of our baby by a surgical procedure; she wanted to see him. More than that: she felt an urgent need to protect him from harm.

So I had to ask myself: Why didn't I want to meet my own son? Clearly, it wasn't Lisa's pain I was worried about. We pulled into the driveway, phoned the hospital, turned around, drove back.

■   ■   ■

Going to the hospital for a stillbirth is the photographic negative of going for a live birth. You bring the overnight bag, check into a room in the maternity ward, and so on. But they put a marker on your door, a picture of a teddy bear with a blue ribbon, to alert the nurse-midwives that, in this room, things are different.

As a means of inducing labor in a body that is not yet ripe, Pitocin is brutally effective, but it can take a while to kick in. After an hour of flipping through magazines, Lisa and I decided to take a walk. The nurse said it might speed things along.

Wandering about in the midwinter dusk, Seattle sinking to the bottom of the gray scale, we were about a quarter mile from the hospital, just about to turn around, when the drug took hold, doubling Lisa over. We considered calling a cab, but she decided she could make it, so we stumbled back with her arm around my shoulders for support.

By the time we reached Lisa's room, her contractions were frequent and prolonged—much more so than they would have been at the early stages of a natural labor—and each surge of pain seemed to levitate her body above the sheets. When at last the anesthesiologist gave her an epidural, Lisa sighed and fell back into the pillows. Within an hour, she was asleep, and shortly after that, like a Labrador curled up in the armchair at the foot of her bed, I dozed off as well. All night, through the walls came the muffled sounds of other women in various stages of labor and, now and then, the distant cry of a newborn.

■   ■   ■

James was born sometime in the gray dawn. In such cases, there is no rupturing of waters. The birth sac slips out whole and unbroken. The bag was a little bigger than the size of my fist. The midwife put it on a towel and, with a small pair of scissors, carefully snipped it open.

She unfolded our son's limbs, disentangling one from the other, unfurling him like a new leaf, talking softly to us all the while, describing him. It's a boy, she said. He's about five inches long. He's anencephalic, which means his brain and nervous system failed to develop. He probably died about a week ago.

Gingerly, she handed him to me. Resting on my outstretched hand, he was thin, nearly weightless, his skin pinkish-gray, translucent. Though the mask of his face was perfectly composed, I could see that the back of his head had not fully formed. He seemed to me less like a small baby than a scale model of a stripling child. I cradled his head between the ends of my middle and ring fingers, his features peaceful, perfect, blank. His feet reaching nearly to my wrist, his toes were like mine and my father's, the second toe longer than the big toe.

The midwife left us alone so that we could say goodbye to him. Not knowing what else to do, I passed him to Lisa. She held him, not as she would have held a baby in her arms—he was too small and delicate for that—but as she might have cradled an injured sparrow in her palm. After all that she had been through to see him, I thought Lisa would spend more time with James, but after only a minute or two she asked me to call for the midwife. Later, Lisa told me he had looked so fragile that she was afraid he would come apart in her hand. Carefully handing his body back to the midwife, Lisa asked her to promise to look after him, to see that he was treated with respect.

When we got back from the hospital, the epidural had not quite worn off, so Lisa did not have full use of her legs and clung to me as we staggered up the front steps. Thinking of ourselves as a public spectacle—How must we look to the neighbors? Drunk again!—first Lisa, then I started to laugh, and then we couldn't stop: Anencephalic? All right, so he won't go to Harvard.

It wasn't until I had settled Lisa on the couch that my own legs quit working. I was midsentence—something about an errand—teakettle in hand, halfway between the tap and the stove. A spasm went through me, I doubled over, and I heard my own voice howling from far off, the full-throated cry of a child.

11.

For the first week after James's birth, Lisa and I stayed home together; we could hardly bear to talk to anyone but each other. We called our respective bosses, explained the circumstances, and asked them to let our students know that we would be back as soon as possible. We told our parents and a few close friends, but apart from that inner circle, hardly anyone knew that Lisa had been pregnant in the first place. This created an insurmountable, absurd difficulty—a "good news/bad news" story so wild that we couldn't imagine trying to tell it to anyone else.

And so, there we sat, in our partly renovated house with our private grief. The nurses at the hospital had referred us to counselors and social workers. They gave us a list of books to read and websites to visit. It's not that there aren't resources available to people who have had similar experiences. Whatever your ache, loss, or unfulfilled desire may be, you'll find people out there on the web who have banded together. Need someone to talk to? There are meetings to attend, phone numbers to call.

We availed ourselves of none of these resources. It just did not occur to us to do so, any more than it would occur to a man who has just been struck by lightning to drag himself, clothes still smoking, to a support group. We sat very still on the couch, the clock ticking on the mantelpiece. Sleep was a relief. To be awake was to look inward, constantly trying to assess the damage.

The hospital released James's body to the funeral home, and a few days later we went there to arrange for his cremation. The young man who helped us seemed just out of college. Wearing a cheap tie and an ill-fitting suit, it was clear that he hadn't had much experience. Thinking perhaps that he could somehow normalize the situation, he tried to draw us into pleasant conversation. I nodded and said a few things in return, trying to put him at his ease, but Lisa just stared at him. Even under the best of circumstances, my wife does not suffer fools gladly, and it was plain that she wanted to kill him. Still chattering nervously, he showed us into a room that clearly had been designed for large groups, extended families, to gather and plan elaborate services. Seating us at the enormous conference table, he offered us coffee. I declined politely as Lisa sobbed. After a moment, I suggested he should probably just get us the forms to sign.

He excused himself, and we sat quietly for a while, just the two of us, staring at the vast expanse of table before us. Off to our left, a display case featured a selection of urns. Religious urns, urns for two, marble urns, shiny metal urns, biodegradable urns. One had a motorized revolving top with a little landscape: boulders, a gnarled tree, and a bald eagle with wings outstretched. The motor made a little whirring sound, and with each revolution, the urn emitted a series of tiny squeaks, as if the mechanism were in need of a spot of WD-40. We burst out laughing.

We had not quite contained ourselves by the time the young man returned with the forms. He stopped short in the doorway, as if he had somehow blundered into the wrong room. I waved him in, and, my shoulders still shaking, I signed the form authorizing James's cremation on the blank labeled *father*. It was the first time anyone had referred to me as a father, and I wondered whether it would be the last.

.   .   .

How do you go about grieving for someone who never lived outside the womb? How do you even *start*? However sudden and terrible a death in the family may be—a spouse, a parent, a sibling—there are rituals to follow, and a linear progression of tasks. First thing is to let people know, and there is a script to follow: you tell them you have bad news; you tell them what happened; they say, "I'm so sorry"; and you say, "Thank you." They send flowers. They bring food. They put on sober costumes and they donate to a designated charity. They offer a handshake or an embrace and ask, in low tones, if there's anything they can do. At the memorial service, they gather to remember, to pay tribute, to comfort. But also, they gather to send the family on their way—the dead to the earth, or to the next life; the living to traverse the arid and seemingly featureless territory ahead.

Like love, grief comes upon us; it happens to us. As with any force that acts on us, we may resist it or we may surrender to it, but either way it changes us and it changes everything around us. The rituals of bereavement, however rote they may be, help us to recognize these changes. They orient us to the new landscape, and they point the way through difficult terrain. As we set out, we become agents in our own lives, not just passive receptacles for grief, but people who *grieve*.

Lisa and I tried to figure out some way to create a memorial for James, to gather our friends around us, not just to mark his passing but to find some public way simply to acknowledge that he had existed. But neither of us, on our own, could imagine any ritual that would feel both right and appropriate. And when we tried to come up with something together, our lack of a common set of religious beliefs—and the shared language that comes with them—made for treacherous negotiations and painful misunderstandings.

Not that, had we both been Catholic, say, or Jewish, there would have been an easy answer to our dilemma. While some priests and rabbis have been known to create special services for grieving parents, neither religion has an official liturgy for stillbirth.

The American way of death includes no acknowledgment of the stillborn. For all the shouting we do at one another about when life begins, we've lost our ability to comfort one another when it slips away so early. Not only is there no ritual, there is no conversation. When you ask a woman how many children she has, she doesn't say, as women were once able to, simply, "I have seven, four living." In this society, so violent and yet so unversed in grieving, you can't drop death into a casual conversation; telling the simple truth becomes an assault.

■   ■   ■

A week after James's birth, I went back to work, but Lisa remained at home. It wasn't only that she needed time to physically recover; she wasn't ready to be out in a world where people were moving about as if nothing had happened. Though I had a similar dread of facing the workaday world, I was more frightened by my own immobility. Ready or not, I wanted to be back on my feet.

Driving down the interstate, then walking across the University campus to my office, I felt myself in a kind of altered state, not above the flow of daily life but just below it, heavy, settled, still.

There is a deeper reality, just under this one: like Everyman, we are, all of us, on a pilgrimage to the end of the world; and we know it, but it's hard to remember. Certainly, the very ill and the very old remember; perhaps people who pray remember more often; and then, there are people who grieve. When you grieve, you remember. This remembering puts a distance between you and those who are not grieving. The language of their country is not the language of your country. You become a stranger passing through, and you are on fire. Everything is on fire.

I taught my first class of the day without incident, but soon afterward I found myself in my office, the door closed, staring blankly at the backlog of e-mail on my computer screen. I realized I couldn't carry on the pretense that nothing had happened, but neither could I face going from office to office and dropping the dead weight of the story on each of my friends and coworkers in turn.

I had to let people know somehow, so I composed an e-mail saying simply that our son, James, had been stillborn last week and asking people to hold us in their hearts. I intended to send it only to the people I had told about the pregnancy, but then I couldn't remember which people I had told and which I hadn't. Sitting paralyzed, my hands motionless on the keyboard, I grew more and more frustrated. Finally, I clicked on the e-mail program's address book and sent the message to everyone at the University: faculty, staff, students, people I knew, people I had never met, people I would never meet, everyone.

Some people were offended, I know. No one told me so directly, but my department's administrative assistant said later that she received a few e-mails asking who the hell I was. And I'm sure there were others who felt it was inappropriate to broadcast such personal news via mass e-mail. I thought it was inappropriate too, but given that the only alternative seemed to be silence, I was too angry to care.

And then came the outpouring: for weeks after, people I barely knew would come into my office, gently shut the door behind them, and burst into tears. I heard stories of single and serial miscarriages, stillbirths, pregnancies carried nearly to full term—all the lost, lost children. Griefs hauled about with nowhere to put them down. Some said they had never told anyone. Who would understand?

12.

We retrieved James's ashes, about a teaspoonful in a small gold box, from the funeral home. When she was well enough, as if she could burn through her grief and rage by sheer physical effort, Lisa crashed around the garden by herself, not yet planting, but tearing up the matted ground, ripping out weeds, hauling around stones and soil, shoveling compost in the freezing March drizzle. We talked about setting aside part of the garden as a memorial, but, to Lisa, the expanse of land behind our house felt too big, too cold, and too far away for such a small soul. To keep him close, she put the box in the drawer of her nightstand.

I suppose that everyone grieves in different ways and at different rates. I wish I could say that we did it together, but it's hard for two people to keep pace with one another on such a difficult and bewildering route. So, as Lisa stomped around the garden, I threw myself into my work.

At the time, I was scheduled to begin rehearsals for a production of *Everyman* at the University. Written at the very end of the fifteenth century, the play is a series of comic, though increasingly painful, abandonments. Once Everyman has been touched by Death and embarks on his pilgrimage, he finds time and again that he has lost his connection with everyone he has ever known. The world has not changed, but Everyman has. He runs to his closest friend (Fellowship) for help, but Everyman comes to see that Fellowship is both cowardly and shallow. Everyman's family (Kindred and Cousin) barely recognize him. The figure representing Everyman's worldly Goods not only refuses to go with him to the grave but reveals that he has intentionally misled Everyman all these years.

Everyman turns to the sacraments for relief, and there he finds some comfort. But when he nears the grave, Everyman suffers the worst betrayals as his body and mind begin to deteriorate. His Beauty refuses to go with him to the grave, and then his Strength. His Discretion proves unreliable. In the final insult, he loses his Five Wits. Blind, deaf, fading, failing, he cries out to God that all have forsaken him. But he is mistaken: Good Deeds stays with him, taking that final long walk, and standing with him in his hour of Judgment, when everyone and everything else has vanished.

All of which, I realize, makes it sound like this was a production you would not want to attend. At least not on a date. But the play appealed to me, not as a means of inflicting my particular grief on the audience (I've suffered for my art; now it's your turn), or haranguing them about materialism and greed, but as a way to gather people, as a reminder that we are on this brief, bright pilgrimage together. I could find no way to publicly mourn the death of my son. But like Everyman on his frantic journey, in the end, in this strange land, I just wanted the solace of company.

I had an idea that the audience should actually walk with Everyman, so, rather than performing the play in a theater, we staged it outdoors, in modern dress, and set each scene in a different campus location. In between the scenes, the actor playing Everyman (who wore the baggy sweats and backward baseball cap of a college student) would dash off to the next location, and the audience would follow on foot—walking about a mile in the course of the evening—accompanied by a small marching band playing Dixieland.

The actors, the designers, and I agreed that a play in fifteenth-century verse in which the main character dies (and not just once, at the end, but at the *beginning* as well) had grimness to spare—the show had to be surprising and funny. The play starts with God (I cast a woman in the role) lamenting that Everyman has forgotten about Her. So, we had the audience gather in a field next to a wooded area where we had rigged up some zip lines among the trees, and all through the first speech of the play, we had angels (little girls in prom dresses with wings attached to their backs) go flying by, shouting, "Whee!"

We wanted to have some fun with the idea that Everyman was a college student. Fellowship, we decided, would live in the dorms. All through his scene with Everyman, we had a loud party in progress on one of the upper floors; from time to time, a beer can or an item of intimate apparel would sail over the balcony railing and land at the audience's feet. When Everyman called his relatives for help (on a cell phone), they drove up in an suv. Five actors dressed as college cheerleaders, speaking and gesturing in unison—and moving in elaborately choreographed routines—played Everyman's Five Wits.

On the last leg of the journey, in the fading light, we passed out candles to the audience, and, as we all walked with Everyman on a path through the dark woods, from the monastery to the monk's graveyard, we sang a call-and-response hymn. We timed the show so that it would end just as the sun set behind the tracery of Douglas firs at the back of the cemetery. In the fading light, the cast lit sparklers and hoisted one of the angel girls on their shoulders, as she welcomed Everyman to heaven.

At the very end, as if she were a valedictorian delivering a commencement address, a student dressed in a graduation gown stepped forward to deliver the play's final speech. As is traditional in New Orleans funerals, the band, who had waited outside the cemetery gates, then struck up a lively jazz tune as a recessional—if you listened closely, as the band walked away from the graveyard, you could hear the trombone weave in a phrase or two of "Pomp and Circumstance." As valedictorians are fond of overbrightly reminding us, the word *commencement* means beginning.

What they don't mention is that the word *valedictorian* means "one who says farewell."

13.

Within hours of giving birth to James, Lisa's nausea and fatigue had lifted, and she felt that her body had been returned to her. Within days of absorbing the initial impact of his death, she determined that she would get the rest of her life back as well. As February blurred into March, Lisa would note, each day, in her appointment calendar, various measures of her progress toward normalcy: whether she'd had any residual bleeding; whether the day was good, bad, or just okay; her declining weight; the duration and intensity of her physical exercise; her accomplishments in the garden. By April, she was also tracking her menstrual cycles, and, with the doctors' assurance that James's death was the result, not of any genetic anomaly, but of plain bad luck, we resumed our visits to the fertility clinic. In May, on the day she came to see the final performance of *Everyman*, Lisa got pregnant.

Jackpot; here we go again.

As with James, Lisa was unremittingly ill for the entire first trimester and beyond, and, once again, my work on the house took on a sense of urgency, not just because I was racing the gestational clock but because, once again, Lisa was too ill to do much of anything herself.

In June, she abandoned her system of labeling the days in her calendar simply as good or bad. On the inside cover of her calendar, she scrawled an Ashleigh Brilliant aphorism: "I try to take one day at a time, but sometimes several days attack me at once." According to urban legend, the Inuit language has the capacity to make exquisitely fine distinctions among many types of snow; likewise, Lisa decided she would need a wide variety of descriptors for her bad days, among them: ill, nauseated, depressed, unhappy, weary, stressed, low-energy, difficult, sick, exhausted, and awful.

In July, the fatigue remained but the nausea eased. Among the bleak entries in Lisa's calendar, like a snippet of birdsong, the occasional "Good day!" Like carrier pigeons returning from a mission, the pounds Lisa had lost were welcomed back one by one and logged in. Unable to track any other particular accomplishments of her own besides remaining pregnant, Lisa took to keeping a meticulous daily record of my progress on home renovations. Lisa's stepfather and I built a circular brick patio in the backyard, and for entertainment, she would sit there in a lounge chair watching me as I painted the exterior of the house.

By the fall, it was clear that Lisa was growing a healthy and extremely active (it was hard to get him to stay still long enough to get a good ultrasound picture) baby boy.

Benjamin. Trying to imagine what he was up to in there, Lisa pictured him variously as swimming laps, shooting hoops, and rearranging canned goods on his pantry shelves. We reached the second trimester, then passed the ominous twenty-week mark, and, for a brief time, began to believe that this might be a normal pregnancy and that, at the end of January, we would end up with a living child.

Then a series of worries unfolded in nightmarish slow motion, all having to do with the placenta. The first worry was its location: in a small number of cases—and by now we were woefully accustomed to being one of a small number of cases—the placenta situates itself close to or completely covers the cervix, effectively blocking the exit and making a vaginal delivery impossible. Sometimes, as the pregnancy advances and the uterus expands, this condition resolves itself. By mid-September, this was in fact what happened, but the plodding drumbeat of worry about our baby's lifeline continued: now the midwife was concerned about the placenta's *shape*. Normally, the placenta is flat and broad, creating a large area of vascular contact with the uterine wall. "It should resemble a pancake," she said to Lisa, "but what you've got here looks more like a bun."

Of course, we didn't care whether the thing resembled a freaking croissant so long as it continued to function. But having a bun-shaped placenta (again, in a small number of cases) can lead to the fetus being undernourished. Or it can lead to weird and dangerous episodes of high blood pressure in the mother. Or gestational diabetes, which is just as bad as it sounds. Or, it can indicate a slightly higher than normal chance of placental abruption—when all or part of the placenta suddenly separates from the uterine wall. Lisa was twenty-two weeks along. "If you start bleeding," said one nurse, "go straight to the emergency room. Don't go to Labor and Delivery; there won't be anything they can do for your baby."

■   ■   ■

In mid-October, at twenty-six weeks, in the middle of the night, part of the placenta did indeed come loose. A rush of bright arterial blood; the call to 911; Lisa lying on the bathroom floor with huge firefighters and paramedics in full gear standing over her; the ambulance ride to the hospital. Within the hour, Lisa was on the operating table surrounded by doctors prepped to perform an emergency C-section. A nurse helped me into a set of surgical scrubs. Fortunately, they stopped the bleeding in time; in that hour, I could easily have lost both my wife and my second son. Had Benjamin been born by caesarean section, at that point, his odds of surviving would have been about fifty-fifty, his odds of surviving without serious, permanent impairment, much lower. Noticing that I looked a little wobbly on my feet, the nurse steered me to a chair.

Lisa spent the next six weeks in the hospital, on constant alert for any sign of fetal distress. For the first several days, the doctors kept her on magnesium sulfate, which inhibits involuntary muscular movements—such as premature contractions—but has the side effect of inhibiting or impairing voluntary muscular movements as well, with the result that the patient lies prone, the body sandbagged, the eyes unable to hold steady and therefore seeing double or triple, the mind racing.

Some of the doctors and nurses tried to reassure us—Lisa happened to be in one of the best hospitals in the world for the care of premature babies, and each day without incident improved the odds of a healthy birth—but the odds had been in our favor before, when Lisa was pregnant with James. We were not disposed to trust in the odds. Even as Lisa stayed on bed rest, even with the full resources of a modern hospital, there was still the real possibility that the placenta could tear again, or come loose entirely, and that we would soon be grieving another child.

At first, the doctors issued strict and specific criteria for Lisa's movement: for a maximum of three hours per day, she was allowed to sit upright in bed or, if need be, to move slowly about the room, take a shower, etc. Once per day, she was allowed to walk down the hall to the common kitchenette. Otherwise, she was to remain, reclining or semireclining, in bed. Not an easy regimen, but at least an unambiguous one.

However, after the first two weeks passed without another bleed, Lisa started receiving contradictory advice from the round-robin of her attending physicians. One told her that she really should stay in bed as much as possible: if she were to have another abruption, it would likely be a bad one, and she should be mentally prepared to be in the operating room within minutes. Another strongly cautioned her about the deleterious effects of long bed rest. He listed the possible consequences: kidney stones, urinary tract infections, loss of muscle mass and bone density. In a tone that implied her tenure in bed was the result of laziness, he urged moderate exercise. How much? "Well, if you start bleeding, then discontinue the exercise." He wrapped up the session by suggesting that, if Lisa remained in the hospital much longer, our HMO might stick us with the bill.

It wasn't just that the doctors were contradicting each other; sometimes, from one day to the next, a doctor would contradict *himself*. (Yes, the attending physicians were all men.) The net effect of their advice was that Lisa should be completely immobile as she exercised, and that she should, without leaving the hospital, go home. "So, what they're saying is, you should jump up and down," I said to Lisa in my best imitation of the doctors' typical bedside manner, "and if you bleed to death, then we'll all know that was the wrong decision."

We soon realized that, however much we wanted a clear prognosis from the attending physicians, we had reached that medical no-man's-land known as, "However certain they may sound, your doctors don't know shit." Accordingly—until such time as two doctors might *agree* on a course of action (which, we realized, still would not constitute *knowing*, but it would be *something*)—we resolved to accept only the most conservative advice, to keep Lisa in the hospital as long as possible and, if necessary, to do battle with our HMO.

Each day after work, when I came to visit Lisa, I would bring her chocolate and brush her hair while she sobbed. Later, when she could no longer bear to stay in bed every sleeping and waking moment, I'd get her a wheelchair and we would go for late-night rambles, spelunking the hospital complex's subterranean corridors. Then I'd tuck her back in bed and return to the construction site that was our house—tarps, paint, and dust everywhere; I didn't even turn on the heat.

By Thanksgiving, the doctors agreed that the placenta seemed to have healed completely. Any chance of another abruption? Well. Yes. Probably not. No. But maybe. Anyway, you should go home, they said.

And how Lisa wanted to. But home was at least half an hour's drive from the hospital. Not close enough. So a friend of ours, Gabriella, who lived a few blocks from the hospital, offered to put us up for as long as we needed. We moved Lisa out of the hospital, and we stayed at Gab's house, bless her, for a month.

By Christmas, at last, the placenta had attained pancake status, and the doctors, to a man, were confident there would be no further mishap. Lisa's Christmas present that year—and mine—was that she got to come home. By mid-January, I was almost done painting the ceiling of our newly finished basement. I had only one small corner to fill in, and I was standing, brush in hand, when Lisa's waters broke, and she called out for me.

14.

Lisa's journal reads, "I had a normal experience—quiet and peaceful (except me—I was yelling)."

If anything so painful and so hazardous can be called normal, I suppose Lisa's labor was at least within hailing distance of normal. But then, I'm a man, so what do I know? Like many of our generation, Lisa and I had done the reading on natural childbirth, and so—even after her previous experience with labor—we still had a certain idealized vision of what the experience might be: drug-free, in specially designed warm-water tubs, soft music playing, the allopathic male doctors at bay (but on alert in case of emergency), a band of wise women and their acolytes applying soothing herbal remedies, and so on. It's a nice story, and we clung to it as long as we could.

I'd heard plenty of stories that weren't so nice. A lot of women I know who have given birth seem to have an overbearing desire for men to understand the degree of pain involved. Sooner or later, grasping for an apt metaphor, they inevitably ask their hapless listener to imagine trying to pass a bowling ball through his penis—or perhaps having his testicles whacked with a large mallet. "That's it!" they cry, a fierce gleam dawning in their eyes. "Picture if you will . . ."

When several women start swapping birth stories, things tend to escalate. One time, in the cafeteria at work, many years before I'd even considered becoming a father, I found myself in the middle of an impromptu session so harrowing that, overcome by queasiness, I had to excuse myself from the table, much to the amusement of my female colleagues. "Oh, don't leave now," they crooned at my retreating back. "We're just getting started."

Despite my erratic driving, Lisa and I made it to the hospital without incident, and with Lisa comfortably installed in a room on the labor and delivery floor, I had time to go back home to retrieve some things we'd forgotten to bring. By the time I returned, Lisa's contractions were consistent with everything we'd heard about the onset of active labor: about five minutes apart and lasting no more than half a minute or so. So far, so good.

However, by early afternoon, the time between contractions shrank to nil. Continuous, unabated, and powerful, each wave of pain rose, crested, and—at last—ebbed slightly, only to be succeeded immediately by the next. In the face of such an incessant onslaught, none of the more idyllic methods for easing a laboring mother's distress were of any use to Lisa. Sitting in the Jacuzzi or on the big bouncy ball made her pain worse, as did lying, in any position, on the bed. The routines she and I had practiced in birthing classes seemed ludicrously out of sync with the reality of nonstop contractions. Nevertheless, at the urging of our midwife, we tried doing the one where the laboring woman puts her arms around her partner's neck, and the partner (for reasons I still can't quite fathom) counts the seconds and offers sincere, though clueless, compliments on how well she is doing. After a minute or two of this, Lisa just growled and flung me aside like a rag doll.

She careened around the room, standing upright, doubling over, lurching from the bed to the wall and back. Finally Lisa seized a small, flimsy metal table that proved to be just the right height to support her as she stood bent over at the waist, moaning and rocking from side to side. Fearing that the table would collapse, I grabbed hold of the other side of it and tried to hold it steady. This went on for quite some time. At one point, I leaned over and suggested that she might perhaps consider grabbing onto something the same height but more stable (such as the bedstead, for example, which I helpfully pointed out was *right next to her*), but Lisa just snarled and continued her death grip on the table.

For some of the time, we had a doula in attendance who gave her massages, but besides destroying hapless furniture, very little else helped Lisa ease the pain. I certainly wasn't much help. I anchored the table and fed Lisa some ice chips now and again, but, most of the time, standing there, buffeted by the storm of Lisa's farmyard expostulations, I was about as useful as tits on a bull.

After twelve hours of this, when the midwife examined her cervix, Lisa had only progressed from 1.5 centimeters to three. It was after midnight, and I think Lisa might have just kept going if everyone in the room with her didn't look utterly exhausted. She wondered aloud whether she should maybe get an epidural, and the midwife, in her understated way, said she thought that might be a good idea.

■　　■　　■

The epidural is a direct line to the lower spinal cord. A steady drip of anesthetic shuts down the south end of the neural superhighway, allowing only a trickle of communication through to the brain and effectively rendering the laboring mother a paraplegic. The contractions continue, but the lower body is on its own expedition, sending back only the occasional blurred dispatch. Once the drugs kicked in, it was as if we had arrived, blinking and disoriented, in the sunshine and sudden silence at the eye of the hurricane.

It was only then that I noticed they'd put us in the room right next door to where Lisa gave birth to James.

Once again, as I had eleven months before, I curled up on a couch beside the bed and caught a few hours' sleep. Exhilarated, after all these years, to be in labor with a full-term child, and terrified that if she nodded off, even for a moment, she might have another bleed without realizing it, Lisa sat up all night, hands on her belly, a sentinel, watching over her boy.

■　　■　　■

By early morning, she had only progressed to five centimeters, and we were bracing ourselves for another long haul. But when a nurse examined her again just before noon, she said Lisa had reached nine centimeters, and—no hurry, whenever she felt like it—she could start pushing. "Yep," said the nurse, "I think you'll meet your baby before 1:00 P.M." So it was that Lisa found suddenly that she, by God, *did* want to push, and with our doula both steadying and coaching her, she squatted on the bed and bore down.

A man would be foolhardy to compare his wife to a Boeing 747, but an hour later, as I stood at the foot of the bed, and Lisa, in the final stage now, lay back, I felt very much as if I were standing at the end of an airport jetway, holding a hand-lettered cardboard sign, waiting for a relative I'd never met to emerge. The midwife set up a mirror so Lisa could watch as the baby's head crowned, slid back, and crowned again.

Then things started moving very fast.

The midwife asked me to put my hand on the top of the baby's head while she summoned the neonatal resuscitation team. "Just hold him in there for a sec while we get ready, okay?" And I said, "Sure," as if physically preventing a baby from sliding out of my wife's womb was something I did every other Thursday. The nurses gathered around, and as I took my hand away, my son's scalp emerged, his forehead, his eyes—he was looking wildly from side to side as if to say, "Where AM I?"—and then the long, long rest of him. In the tumult of birth, the umbilical cord had wrapped itself twice around his neck. The midwife unwound and cut it, and the nurses rushed him to the other side of the room where they suctioned out his airway. And all the time, Lisa's calling out to me: "Tell me what's going on! Is he okay? Is the baby okay?" And I'm just standing there dumbstruck because I have no *idea* whether he's okay.

And then his first breath, a choking cry, and I saw his body turn from grayish-blue to pink, the blush of oxygenated blood spreading from the chest to limbs as if my son were framed in the center of a black-and-white movie shot irising outward into living color.

A nurse handed him to me and told me to bring him to Lisa so that he could do the "breast crawl." Fortunately, from child-birthing class, I remembered what on earth a breast crawl might be: you put the baby on the mom's belly so that he's got a little distance to cover before discovering the nipple; this helps initiate the breastfeeding process—and, perhaps, by putting the little bugger to work in his very first minute of existence outside the womb, encourages a lifelong habit of industry.

Sure enough, after resting a moment on Lisa's belly, he started creeping along, though, at first, in the wrong direction. "Hello, baby," said Lisa. "*This* way."

Later that evening, as my wife slept, I held him, swaddled tightly in a baby blanket, this ridiculously small person for whom I was now responsible. I stared out the window at the rain, the red glow of the SAFEWAY supermarket sign reflected on the shining pavement—all but two of its letters were burned out: "E-W, ew!" I whispered to my son, the first of many jokes he would neither appreciate nor understand.

Warm, dry, inside, safe, I rocked him, this stranger.

15.

My father wasn't at my birth. Told that my mother was not likely to give birth for some time, he went home to get some rest. I once asked my mother if she resented his absence, and she said no. "It was another time." "Besides," she added, "your father didn't do very well with blood and pain."

Or shit, apparently. When my parents came to see their newborn grandson, and I had Ben on the changing table, my father remarked that he had never changed a diaper. "Great!" I said. "Here's your chance. I'll show you how." He grinned, declined politely, and, as he turned away, told me he wouldn't want to get in the way of my father-son bonding process.

I took paternity leave and, when I wasn't occupied with Benjamin's other end, spent the better part of a month staring at his face. A woman has a head start on such things; feeling the life growing, quickening inside her, she is bonded to her child long before birth. It can take a little longer for a father to fall in love, to become so completely besotted with the appearance of his son that all other faces look hideous by comparison.

I've never finished painting that tiny patch of ceiling I was working on when Lisa's waters broke—instead, I glued a copy of his birth announcement to the spot. Seven pounds, two ounces, twenty inches. My boy.

When I went back to work, for two days straight I had what must have been a separation-anxiety headache. Every chance I got, I would corner hapless colleagues and push baby pictures on them, saying, "Now, is this not a beautiful baby? I mean, I've seen a lot of ugly babies in my time, the ones with pointy heads, squashed faces, and those squinchy expressions, you know the type—like tiny Winston Churchills. But this, *this* is a really extraordinarily beautiful baby!"

My favorite facial expression: when Ben was hungry, he would turn his head from side to side, eyes closed, lips extended, face quivering in happy expectation, as if a breast could be *anywhere*. There, I thought, *there* is one optimistic child: may he always see the world as a place of such abundance, and may he come to believe in a generous, loving God.

So after all my efforts, on the Camino and afterward, to find some spontaneous and unaffected form of prayer, there it was, in that moment, a simple request: a good life for my son. Ever since, when I look at him—especially when he's unaware of my gaze, when he's asleep, or absorbed in some task, or playing with other children—it's not unusual for the prayers for my son to well up in me and overflow. If there's a God, I hope that's how he watches over us, looking when we're not looking, with the aching heart of a hopelessly devoted father.

Actions are prayers too, and as I am trying, not always successfully, to be a good parent, a good husband, a good teacher, I sometimes think: *this* is my conversation with God. It seems to me now that the action of walking to Santiago was, in itself, a prayer—a prayer repeatedly and resoundingly answered. Benjamin is an answered prayer, of course, but so was James. He just wasn't the answer we expected.

I have two sons, one living. I would not now trade the road Lisa and I took for an easier one. Losing James was hard, but I'm thankful that I got to see him, and I am thankful that I got to grieve him as well. As most any pilgrim will tell you, the difficulty of the undertaking is what gives it meaning. All the petty competition for authenticity among the pilgrims on the Camino has its roots in something by no means trivial: pilgrimage is meant to be done the hard way. A real pilgrimage, a real life, contains, and is defined by, difficulty—hardship, and how we respond to it, makes us who we are, certainly more than anything that comes easy.

There are times, for all the tedium and discomfort of the journey, when I miss being on the Camino, not so much for its more pleasant aspects, but for the discipline, the stripping away, piece by piece, of all the blooming, buzzing distractions of modern life, until only the present-tense, animal truth is left: move, eat, drink, sleep—and look to your companions. In its own way, grief does the same. There is a part of grief that goes beyond suffering: a burning, searing cleanliness, a scourging of the quotidian right down to the living bone. And so, though I know it may seem odd, I sometimes miss being in that state of grief too—not the pain of it, but the clarity underneath the pain: after the blinding flash, the seeing through.

But it's a hard to place live, that state of grief, and I don't see that any of us has any choice about whether we remain there or not. Claire still lives there. As Cori and Blake's mother, remembrance has become her life. She says it's like carrying stones. Each day adds another stone to her load, and each day she shoulders that load and moves on, one foot in front of the other.

Last year, Claire opened a mosaic art studio. She teaches workshops and hosts art shows there, but her specialty is in working with people who are grieving; she helps them to design and create memorials. Some of these memorials are quite beautiful; some are never finished. Claire says she's come to understand the value of simply giving people a place to be sad. And there in her studio they sit together, breaking glass, and then slowly and carefully putting the broken pieces together again, forming something new, over and over.

Had Benjamin not been born, I suppose that Lisa and I would eventually have created a memorial in our garden for James, but with the safe arrival of our second son, those plans were put aside; at once, that patch of real estate had other purposes: strawberry plants, a sandbox, a fort with a trap door. We haven't forgotten James's death, but such a sudden abundance of life made us move on.

When Ben was only a week old, Claire came to visit us and brought with her as a gift a soft, striped baby blanket that has become my son's most cherished possession. He still sleeps with it every night. When we draw up a list of what to take with us on any journey longer than half a day, Stripey is right at the top.

One time, when Ben was about three, I left Stripey on a playground park bench, and when I realized an hour later what I had done, without a word, I grabbed Ben, stuffed him in the stroller, and ran back to the playground in abject terror. If I failed to recover my son's beloved transitional object, I knew what the consequence would be: I would no longer be "Daddy." Instead, to this day I would be known as "that guy who lost Stripey."

■ ■ ■

We've accomplished nearly everything on Lisa's master list of renovations. The moldy windows are gone. With Lisa's stepfather's help, I built a structure that began its life as a cedar tool shed but over the years has acquired a stained glass window, inside walls, crown and baseboard moldings, and two secret compartments—one for Lisa and one for Ben. Lisa calculates that, over the past ten years, her various landscaping projects have involved trucking in roughly one hundred cubic yards of compost, leaf mulch, and gravel. The incoherent, gnarled remnants of previous plantings have been removed, and Lisa has created a lush oasis—a secret garden of raised beds, fruit trees, shrubs, and ornamental grasses—surrounded by a cedar fence, thickets of bamboo, and lines of arbor vitae. Our home is as peaceful a refuge as we could want. At least for now, Lisa and I have no desire to travel. All the adventure we need is well within walking distance.

We don't fight much anymore. We have our disagreements, of course, but we generally work them out peacefully, without recriminations or theatrics. Pilgrimage and parenthood—which, for us, for now, have become one and the same—have put our doubts about each other to rest. Lisa has learned to trust me; I've learned to step up. It works pretty well for us. Your results may vary.

16.

On the day he died, one fall morning in 2007, my father, who was just short of his seventy-six birthday, was out doing what my mother and I called his "rounds." He would often disappear in the midmorning or afternoon and take the car without saying where he was going. Sometimes he wouldn't even tell my mother he was leaving the house. My father, so responsible for all his adult life, would, for part of the day, simply run away from home.

He might pick up the newspaper at Stewart's, or stop at the Nibble Nook to have a cup of coffee and trade affectionate insults with the cook and waitress, to eat the greasy food that, as his girth expanded and his blood pressure rose, my mother refused to prepare for him at home. Or he might go see Bill, his broker; he'd drop by the office, ostensibly to ask about some detail of the management of his finances, which were, by his own dictate, and against Bill's persistent entreaties, so conservatively invested that there really wasn't much managing to do. My dad would pour himself another cup of coffee in the reception area (caf or decaf—he said it never affected him one way or the other), and Bill would begin the kidding, charging out of his office hollering, "What? You're here *again*? I do have other clients, you know."

Sometimes my father might do an actual errand, get groceries, or maybe buy something from the hardware store, but for the most part, these trips were neither necessary nor practical. He just liked people, and so he would find excuses to go out and provoke them.

For my father's seventieth birthday, Lisa and I wrote up a list entitled "Seventy Things We Like about You." My dad took it with him on his rounds, and whenever he found himself happily ensconced in an argument, he would pull out the list and show it around. "See," he would say, "seventy things they like about me. It's right here, thirty-two: my common sense. And here, look, this is number four: *my sense of humor.*" When he was about to turn seventy-one, he asked me if Lisa and I were going to send him an addendum, but I told him, "Gosh, Dad, it was so agonizing trying to think of seventy good things about you; I don't think we could possibly come up with one more." Instead, I sent him a bag of exotic fertilizer derived from the excrement of zoo animals. He spent the next week of his rounds bragging that his ungrateful son had sent him a sack of shit for his birthday.

We have no idea where he was off to, the day he was killed. As he was making a left turn from the two-lane county road onto the four-lane state highway, my father misjudged the speed of an approaching car, which hit him broadside. A police detective told me later that, judging from the damage to my father's car, the other driver, who was unhurt, may have been traveling twice the forty-five-mile-per-hour speed limit. What happened to my dad could happen to anyone, the detective said: when you're looking at a car coming toward you straight on, you can't really tell how fast it's going. You think you've got plenty of time, so you pull out and some idiot T-bones you. Why people speed is beyond me, he added. Just racing so they can get stuck at the next traffic light, you know?

No one saw the collision. The owner of a nearby store, who must have heard the crash, called 911. A passerby, who happened to be a nurse, stopped and found my father pinned against the steering wheel of his car, fully conscious, uncomfortable, but not in pain. He asked the nurse to call my mother, who arrived at the scene within minutes.

At first, while the firemen were cutting the car open, they wouldn't let my mother go to him, but once they had put my father on a stretcher, they allowed her a moment with him before they loaded him into the ambulance. She kissed him and told him she loved him. He didn't seem to be badly hurt; she was thinking he'd be fine. She thought she'd go home, pack an overnight bag for him, and meet him at the hospital.

The ambulance pulled away. A fireman asked my mother to look in the wrecked car for any personal possessions my father might want to keep. He told her that my father had been asking for his glasses. After a brief search, she found the glasses, jammed up against the rear windshield, still intact. She wished she had found them before my father was taken away. He hated to be without his glasses.

That would be the last time she saw my father alive. Outwardly, his injuries seemed insignificant, but, as it turned out, the internal damage was past repairing. He died on the operating table.

They had been married fifty-five years.

∎   ∎   ∎

Before he died, my father had nearly six years with Ben, enough time that Ben will remember him, his kindness, his generosity, his wicked sense of humor. When I think about my dad, I imagine how delighted he would be at each milestone of his grandson's development, and when I have a "Ben story" I know he'd love, I miss him. And, to me, that remembrance too is a kind of prayer.

Ben is eight years old now, tall for his age, slim, and in constant motion. He loves horses, draws enormous pictures of saltwater crocodiles, often imagines he is a garden elf, and—seeking raw materials for his inventions—regularly pillages our recycling bin. He is still young enough to be interested in being with his parents. He and I have epic wrestling matches, shouting at each other in pseudo-Samurai gibberish. I lose every time. On our bicycles, we explore the streets surrounding our house as if each block were a distant and exotic country. Lisa and I are gradually introducing him to all the things on my "incentive" list: he took to cake and hummingbirds right away, and though it seems he's not quite ready to appreciate Otis Redding, when I put on "Sam and Dave's Greatest Hits," he dances around the living room with a goofy abandon that puts gracefulness to shame.

You might suspect that, after all the difficulty we went through to get Benjamin here, we would be anxious parents, but I don't think we are, at least not unduly. He is fine; through it all, as I often remind myself, Benjamin has always been just fine. In this story, as in so many of our stories these days, he is the happy ending.

Each day, I try to remind myself that none of this, and none of us, will last forever. Now is the time to hold him close, but when it comes time for Benjamin to strike out on his own, my hope is to let my son go as gracefully as my father launched me. When I was nineteen, in the middle of college and desperately in love with a girlfriend who had left me to travel overseas, I told my parents I wanted to use my savings and take a leave of absence so I could join her. Needless to say, they disapproved, but rather than censuring me or threatening to withhold his financial support for my education, my father told me that I should do what I thought was right. If I needed it, he added, he'd always pay the airfare—from anywhere in the world—for me to come home.

It's been three years now since my father's death, and though she doesn't like to talk about it, I know that my mother still mourns him, so I call or write to her every day. I bring Benjamin to see her whenever I can; they can't get enough of each other.

It's been ten years since Lisa and I returned from the end of the world, our backpacks full of scallop shells, our faces (judging from the photographic evidence) still impossibly youthful. We are, as I write this, in the year 2010, in this brief moment of happiness. The hard fact of its impermanence—when I can bring it to mind—makes me all the more thankful. And though I imagine I will always be a restless person, now that we have finally reached, by a pretty hard road, the land of parenthood, I do find myself more appreciative of—more apt to find the miraculous in—the ordinary. In this land where the days are endless and the years fly by, where I make mistakes all the time, and where there is a love beyond language, I find that I am content to put down my pack and stay a while.

EPILOGUE (2015)

I'm now well past my fiftieth birthday, the age at which a man looks in the mirror and sees his own father ever more clearly, and at which he can feel the increase of gravity, in ways both subtle and unsubtle, that comes as the ground gets steeper on the downward path to the grave. But I am enjoying my life now more than I ever did before, because lately the happy ending—in what I thought was this book's final chapter—just keeps getting better, not just for me but for the people I love.

My mom, who, at eighty-two, is something of a force of nature, continues to thrive and bloom. She has her down days like anyone, and she misses my father, but she's set up a community organization for the elderly and disabled who want to remain in their homes; they share resources and skills (the ones who can drive take others who can't on shopping trips, for example). She's preparing a collection of her poetry for publication. We still e-mail each other daily, and when she and Ben get on the phone together, they chat for hours. Ben and I visit her a few times a year; he loves his time with his grandma.

And Claire and Marj: this year, now that the law in our state has, at last, officially realized the obvious rightness and goodness of such unions, they got married.

Lisa and I have been together for more than twenty-five years, and now that we've passed the middle of middle age, some things have become clearer to me—and simpler. As it turns out, this story—the story I wrote four years ago that I once thought was about grief and difficulty—is really about intimacy.

I still love my job. The problem in our early life together wasn't that I was working too much. It was that I was working desperately to advance my career—not a bad thing in itself, but, ultimately, a hollow one. I don't care about my career anymore; I care about the people I work with. I've known some of my coworkers almost as long as I've known my wife. Some of them are retired, and some that I have loved dearly have died. I was a Young Turk when they hired me; now, I'm part of the Old Guard, a graybeard, one of the long-tenured and judicious people they pick to sit on the weighty committees. The big secret is that, despite our collective gravitas and the seriousness of our deliberations, it is in these committees where we have the best time teasing one another, as old friends and true companions do. It's not that I didn't love the people in my work life before Lisa and I walked four hundred miles, lost James, and took on the challenges of building a real home together; it's just that these days, after all that struggle, the reason I leave home to go to work is to relish these close relationships with—and to be of service to—my students and my colleagues.

Lisa has cut back to teaching only one yoga class a week—this after a career that has included publishing a book, teaching at national conferences, and founding a series of events that raised hundreds of thousands of dollars for cancer research. She might have stopped teaching altogether, but the thirty people who come to her Saturday morning class are her regulars, some of whom have studied with her for two decades. It's not that she couldn't have continued working on a grander scale and kept things in perspective. My sense is that, for her, having a career has always been about relationship and service, and this one class is more satisfying to her than any accolades she's earned in the past or might earn in a busier future. Apart from Saturday mornings, Lisa has decided she'd rather not be busy at work; she'd rather be home, busy with Ben. Financially, it makes our life on the lean side at times, but that's okay with us.

In terms of our relationship, when I stopped trying to get the girl—and instead turned my attention to pleasing the one I'd already got—things got a whole lot sweeter. What loving Lisa means in practice, it turns out, is not candlelit dinners for two nor romantic tropical vacations. Instead, it means doing a fair amount of housework and childcare. Buy Lisa flowers, and they just end up in the compost bucket. But take out the compost bucket and dump it in the bin without her asking me to do it: *that*, it turns out, is romantic. Ask a straight woman of a certain age who is trying to balance home, family, and work what her fantasy is, and the sexual is she will describe will most likely involve a man wearing a tool belt or pushing a vacuum cleaner. When I do these good deeds for Lisa, she praises me, and she is, in return, more physically affectionate—which, Everyman that I am, is how I know that I am loved.

Like me, Benjamin thrives on physical contact. Each night, to let him know how much we love him, we gather for a pig pile on Benjamin's bed, a bed far too small to reasonably accommodate all three of us. After we're done shoving each other and complaining about the other two taking up too much room, we talk about our favorite parts of the day. Sometimes, our favorite parts are the things we got done on our own, but more often what we remember is something we laughed at together. We call ourselves The Cozy Family. Our family motto is, "Not Too Shabby."

The garden Lisa worked so hard on has been featured in city garden tours, and we've had hundreds of people tromp through it like horticultural peregrinos, admiring her work. Ben, as junior gardener and tour guide, responds to gardening inquiries with assurance and adorable sincerity. Our home, once a seemingly endless drain on our physical and financial resources, is now so much to our liking that sometimes we can hardly stand to leave it.

These days, when Lisa and I go out together, it's not on dates. What we enjoy more is doing really stupid errands together—going to the hardware store, the DMV, that sort of thing. We treat these outings as small adventures, little pilgrimages if you will, and navigate the local traffic with a mock-heroic sense of purpose and derring-do. We make each other laugh; it gives us hope that someday, if we're lucky enough both to survive to the advanced age at which it seems people spend most of their waking hours going to doctors' offices, we'll still have a good time.

Did Lisa and I have to go through all that pain and loss for me to realize what should be so simple, that connection with other people isn't just a good thing, it's the only thing? For my son's sake, and for the sake of his future spouse, I hope not.

Still, it does seem to be that experiencing real grief and loss is somehow necessary to growing up. One way I know this is from teaching acting to college students. Frequently, when I first encounter them in class, my students seem to have no idea how to relate to other actors, to find that vein of emotional truth that is so essential to creating an engaging performance. I try all kinds of things to wake them up, to distract them from their faking, their desire to concoct some odd artificial simulacrum of human behavior, and to get them to focus on just being in relationship, responding honestly to what the other actor on stage is doing, but oftentimes without much success. Then they come back from summer vacation and suddenly, they *get* it; they're not just acting, they're reacting. And when I ask how their summer was, more often than not it turns out that they had a terrible time. Someone close to them died—or they fell in love and had their heart broken that way.

At twelve, Ben is a young man now, so I figure it's my job—my real job now—when I can, to help him figure out what it means to be a stand-up guy, and to figure it out sooner than I did and with less fuss and less disconnection from his feelings and from the people he loves. I don't know how to do that, except by trying (and sometimes failing) to set an example and looking for teachable moments along the way. But Lisa and I can teach him the skills to be self-sufficient and useful to others. So, at the beginning of his summer vacation this year, the three of us put together a list of things Citizen Ben should know how to do by the time he is old enough to vote. To this syllabus, I added a timeline, a visual representation of the next six years, counting down, month-by-month (seventy-two months, give or take), until, at end of summer 2020: liftoff.

Among other things, Lisa and I are teaching him how to join in and take ownership of his part of the life of this household: how to cook, to bake, to clean, to sew, to repair and maintain things, to shop for groceries, to care for the garden. He is not always a willing or cheerful participant in this undertaking—a venture designed both to bind him to and to launch him from the home of his birth, to give him both roots and wings—but that's okay with us. We tell him he'll be more marketable when we're done with him; a guy who can use power tools *and* who does his share of the housework.

"Son, it's okay to be an asshole now and then," I often tell him in my most sagacious professorial voice, "but don't be a dick." And he responds by telling me that I, his father, am both. Which makes me proud. He may have his mother's good looks, but, for better or worse, he has my sense of humor.

■   ■   ■

I have a timeline too. Looking at the actuarial tables, having reached my age, an Everyman in my part of the world can expect to live, on average, another twenty-six years. If I am as average as I assume, and if my life is not cut short the way my father's was, that should be ample time to put my affairs in order.

To that end, a few years ago, I committed to a daily meditation practice, going on retreats and reading everything I could get my hands on about the Buddha and the Eightfold Path. Every morning, I sit very still, and I watch my thoughts, sensations, emotions. Instead of following them where they lead, I try to let them go. As I've been taught to do, I pay particular attention to duration—how fleeting all these passing phenomena are. Some days, I am able, for just a moment or two, to let go of thinking altogether. For what I'm up to now, thinking is, at best, of very limited use. Mostly, it's a pain in the ass. I'm trying to get out of my head; it's lonely in there. Better to reach out instead. In the short time we have, as the Dalai Lama says, it's all about kindness.

And yet meditation, this inward pilgrimage, this getting right in the mind, is done alone—even if you sit in community with others. Trying to let go of the attachment to self is an oddly solitary task. As Woody Guthrie sang: Nobody else can walk it for you; you've got to walk that lonesome valley by yourself.

So, what the heck, last year I went to the shrink and got myself some low-dose antidepressants too; as a friend of mine said to me the other day, that's the ninth part of the Eightfold Path: Right Medication. I'm not sure what's made more difference, the meditation, the medication, or simply the change of heart that's come over me as I've gotten older, but my wife and son say I'm nicer.

This past summer break, I experienced none of the bereavement and anxiety that used to plague me so during vacations. Now that I am no longer a tourist in my own home, now that I'm a full participant in the life of our island paradise, I look forward to vacations.

■   ■   ■

When Ben was four, I decided to revive the production of *Everyman* that I had directed just after James died, and this time, instead of directing it myself, I asked John, the student who had played Everyman the last time, to come back and direct it. This time, I was in the cast: I played Death. John and I decided that after the initial scene with Everyman, I should remain in character and reappear at various times throughout the rest of the play, always somewhere in the background of each scene, just at the edge of the audience's field of vision. At one point, as the audience walked through the woods on the way to the cemetery, I was about fifty yards to the side of the path, plainly visible. Sometimes no one saw me, but more often, someone would catch a glimpse of me, gasp, and point me out to others.

Lisa brought Ben to the show, and I wanted to prepare him, so I explained that I was playing a scary guy, but a good one, and that he shouldn't worry. But I needn't have worried myself. For him, the show was like a game of *Where's Waldo?* in 3-D. And when the audience walked through the woods, I saw Ben catch sight of me, and I heard him shout triumphantly, "There's my DADDY!"

I'm no different from anyone else; I have no reason to believe that I'll actually achieve Enlightenment or that when it comes time for me to die, I won't be just as ignorant, astonished, and incensed about it as Everyman. But I hope that I will have the people I love near me right up to the very end. And I have this dream that, with a lot of practice, when that end actually arrives, I just might be able to do it differently.

In my dream, when Death comes for me, whether I see him from a ways off or whether he drops by quite suddenly, I will be glad to see him in the same way my son was delighted to spot me, the dark but familiar figure in the forest. I will welcome Death like an old friend, and he and I will settle down and assess the number and extent of my kindnesses to others and how I have enjoyed in turn their kindness to me. And Death and I, intimate at last after all my years of trying to keep him at arm's length, will break bread together on the occasion of my departure from the empty, Lenten house of my body.